Special Needs Trust Administration Manual

A Guide for Trustees
2005 Edition

Barbara D. Jackins, Esq.
Richard S. Blank, Esq.
Ken W. Shulman, Esq.
Peter M. Macy, Esq.
Harriet H. Onello, Esq.

People with Disabilities Press Series
Stanley D. Klein Ph.D., Series Editor

iUniverse, Inc.
New York Lincoln Shanghai

Special Needs Trust Administration Manual
A Guide for Trustees
2005 Edition

iUniverse books may be ordered through booksellers or by contacting:

iUniverse
2021 Pine Lake Road, Suite 100
Lincoln, NE 68512
www.iuniverse.com
1-800-Authors (1-800-288-4677)

ISBN-13: 978-0-595-33106-2 (pbk)
ISBN-13: 978-0-595-77894-2 (ebk)
ISBN-10: 0-595-33106-8 (pbk)
ISBN-10: 0-595-77894-1 (ebk)

Printed in the United States of America

ACKNOWLEDGMENTS

The authors thank Linda L. Landry, Esq., and Barbara L. Siegel, Esq., of the Disability Law Center in Boston for their assistance with the public benefits and housing sections of this manual.

We also thank Stanley D. Klein, Ph.D., Series Editor, People with Disabilities Press and Director, DisABILITIESBOOKS.com and Michael Macfarlane for their assistance with the 2005 edition.

ABOUT THE AUTHORS

Barbara D. Jackins practices law in Belmont, Massachusetts. Her practice centers on areas of the law that affect people with disabilities and their families, such as estate planning, Medicaid planning, SSI and other public benefits, guardianship, and trust administration. She has served on the Governors Commission on Mental Retardation Task Force on Public-Private Partnerships. She currently serves on the Board of Directors of the NWW Committee (Newton, MA), an agency that provides community housing for people with disabilities. She is a member of the National Academy of Elderly Law Attorney and a 1978 graduate of Suffolk University Law School.

Richard S. Blank is a member of the firm Rubin and Rudman LLP in Boston, Massachusetts, where he practices in the areas of trust administration and estate planning. He has extensive experience drafting and administering Special Needs Trusts and preserving government benefits. A substantial part of his practice is focused on integrating personal injury settlements into Special Needs Trusts and then administering those trusts. He is a 1987 graduate of Georgetown University Law Center.

Peter M. Macy is a member of Weston, Patrick, Willard & Redding, a professional association located in Boston, Massachusetts. His practice focuses on Medicaid law, guardianship, estate planning and private trustee services. He also is a founder and director of Family Trust of Massachusetts, Inc., a non-profit organization based in Boston that has established a Medicaid-exempt pooled trust for elderly and disabled persons. Mr. Macy has written about Medicaid for the Massachusetts Law Review and speaks regularly in the Boston area about Medicaid and guardianship topics. He earned his J.D. from Boston College Law School and holds graduate degrees in education and theology from Harvard University. He is a member of the Boston Bar Association and the National Academy of Elder Law Attorneys.

Harriet H. Onello practices Elder Law and Family Law in Lexington, Massachusetts. She is the author of a chapter on Planning for Incapacity in a three-volume book entitled *Estate Planning for the Aged or Incapacitated Client in*

Massachusetts, published by Massachusetts Continuing Legal Education, Inc. She participates as faculty for continuing legal education programs and has made a number of community presentations on elder law issues. She received an M.Ed. from Harvard Graduate School of Education and a J.D. from Suffolk University. Ms. Onello is a founding member and immediate Past President of the Massachusetts Chapter of the National Academy of Elder Law Attorneys.

Ken W. Shulman maintains a private, general practice of law in Boston, Massachusetts, with a particular focus on estate planning and related issues for elders and for families who have children with disabilities. He frequently speaks to consumer groups, professionals in the field, and others interested in issues related to aging, disability, advocacy, financial planning, and the preservation of government entitlements. Prior to his individual practice, he was a partner of McCabe, Shulman, Siegel and Rooney in Boston. He has served as a board member for several human service agencies including the Greater Boston ARC. He has also served as a consultant to the Massachusetts Office of Handicapped Affairs, the Disability Law Center, and the Mental Health Legal Advisors Committee, and he currently serves on the Board of Directors of the Massachusetts Chapter of the National Academy of Elder Law Attorneys. Mr. Shulman is a frequent participant in lawyer training sessions sponsored by the Massachusetts Continuing Legal Education organization and a frequent contributor to their publications, having written numerous articles and co-chaired conferences on estate planning and preserving eligibility for public benefits for disabled clients. He is a graduate of Boston University School of Law.

TABLE OF CONTENTS

PREFACE 2005 EDITION

Timing, it seems, is everything. Just after we published this book in October 2004, the Social Security Administration made three important changes to the SSI program rules. These revisions became effective January 1, 2005. This second edition reflects these changes, which are:

- Clothing is no longer considered in-kind income. Formerly, if an SSI recipient received any clothing from a third party (including a Special Needs Trust), his SSI benefit might be reduced. This is because clothing (along with food and shelter) was considered in-kind income. Now the trustee's job should be easier, because she can use trust funds to pay for the beneficiary's clothes without reducing the SSI benefit. (However, food and shelter are still considered in-kind income that can reduce the SSI benefit.)

- The $4,500 limit on the value of an automobile has been eliminated. Formerly, if an SSI recipient owned an automobile, it had to be worth $4,500 or less, unless it was specially adapted, required for medical transportation, or needed because of distance or geography. Now Social Security disregards the car's value.

- The $2,000 limit on the value of personal items a recipient can own has been eliminated. Formerly, the value of a recipient's personal property (such as furniture, computer, jewelry, etc.) could not exceed $2,000. Now there is no monetary limit on that kind of property. Note, however, that the new law affects only personal items. SSI's strict $2,000 limit on liquid resources (cash, bank account, savings bonds, etc.) remains unchanged.

Besides these important changes, this second edition contains the 2005 figures for all SSI-related examples and calculations. Also, the 2005 figures have been used for all SSI-related programs, including SSDI and Medicaid.

Last, you readers have been very generous with your comments. We have tried to make this second edition responsive to your concerns. For example, apparently there was some confusion about what happens when the Special Needs Trust ends. Some readers erroneously thought the money must always go to the government as a "payback" for the beneficiary's medical benefits. We assure you that this is not the case with every trust. In fact, if the trust was created by someone other than the disabled beneficiary (such as a parent), the money can usually go to other family members (the remainder beneficiaries) when the trust ends. In most cases, government reimbursement is only a factor if the disabled beneficiary uses his own money to fund a trust for himself. This is explained in detail in the revised Chapter One.

Please continue to send us your comments and questions. And thank you all for the positive reception you have given this work.

The Authors

INTRODUCTION

This manual was written for the trustee who is administering a Special Needs Trust for a person with disabilities. It is intended to explain in an uncomplicated, user-friendly way, the rules that govern Special Needs Trusts and how those rules relate to the many complicated government programs that assist people with disabilities. It is directed both to laypersons, such as friends and family of a person with disabilities, and to professionals, including attorneys, financial planners, and social workers—in short, anyone who is administering (or considering administering) a Special Needs Trust.

The authors are all Massachusetts attorneys with many years of practice writing and administering Special Needs Trusts.

In our experience, one of the most commonly asked questions has been, "Is there something I can read?"

Until now, the answer has been "No."

We had nothing to give our clients that explained in a clear, straightforward way their responsibilities as trustees. There was no reference book to help them navigate the complicated rules of government programs that provide money, medical benefits, and housing to people with disabilities. This manual was written to fill that need.

This manual covers such topics as what a Special Needs Trust is, and how trust distributions for medical, recreation, and transportation expenses affect government benefits such as SSI, Medicaid, and housing subsidies. It also discusses the trustee's duties concerning taxes, accounting, final distributions, and the like. Our goal is to help the trustee manage the Special Needs Trust in ways that will enhance the beneficiary's quality of life but not inadvertently violate the complex rules of government benefit programs.

This manual is not an in depth study of SSI, Social Security, or Medicaid laws. Detailed information on those programs can be obtained from the resources listed in the "Where to Go for Help" section of this manual. Nor does this manual attempt to anticipate every situation the trustee might potentially encounter in administering a Special Needs Trust. Rather, this is a practical reference guide that discusses common situations that can arise and how the trustee might address them.

This manual explains how federal law and regulations are applied in Massachusetts. Massachusetts laws, especially in respect to Medicaid, may differ significantly from other states' laws. Thus, trustees outside Massachusetts should work with a local attorney who can guide them through the standards and practices in their state.

Also, program rules and government regulations often change, so it is important to stay current. We will attempt to update this manual periodically to reflect changes in the law. Current information about many public benefits programs and the laws that govern them can be obtained from the websites listed at the end of this manual.

Lastly, this manual is not meant as a substitute for working with an attorney or as legal advice for any particular situation. For that, we recommend that the trustee work with an attorney experienced in public benefits laws, disabilities, and the Special Needs Trust.

RESOURCE MATERIALS

First, a word about the legal references the reader will encounter in this Manual.

Most government programs that assist people with disabilities have been created by federal law and implemented by lengthy and detailed state and federal regulations.

The enabling statute for the Supplemental Security Income (SSI) program is located at section 42 of the United States Code (U.S.C.) §1381, et seq. The regulations that govern that program can be found in section 20 of the Code of Federal Regulations (C.F.R.) §§ 416.101–416.2227. The website is www.ssa.gov.

The enabling statute for the Social Security Disability Insurance (SSDI) program is located at 42 U.S.C.§402, et seq. The federal rules that govern that program can be found at 20 C.F.R., §§404.1–404.2127. The website is www.ssa.gov.

The POMS (Program Operations Manual System) are volumes of guidelines that interpret Social Security laws. These guidelines are relied on by workers at the Social Security local district offices. The POMS, which can provide a wealth of specific examples to guide the trustee, can be found on the Social Security Administration website. That website is www.ssa.gov.

In Massachusetts, the Medicaid rules that govern the MassHealth programs are located in section 130 of the Code of Massachusetts Regulations, (C.M.R.), §§ 500–650. The website is www.lawlib.state.ma.us.

Federal housing program standards discussed in this manual, established by the Dept. of Housing and Urban Development (HUD), are located at 24 C.F.R. §5.609. They can be accessed on www.access.gpo/gov/index.html. Massachusetts housing program rules are located in the Code of Massachusetts Regulations at 760 C.M.R.§5.00. The website is www.lawlib.state.ma.us.

CHAPTER 1

THE SPECIAL NEEDS TRUST

What is a trust?

A trust is an agreement between the creator of the trust (often called the *grantor, donor,* or *settlor*) and a *trustee* to administer (use) property for the benefit of a third party (the *beneficiary*).

The property in the trust can consist of almost any type of asset, including real estate, stocks, cash, bonds, mutual funds, or insurance policies. In order to become part of the trust, property must be transferred to the trustee. For example, in the case of real estate, there must be a deed that names the trustee as the legal owner of the property. A bank or investment account must be registered in the name of the trust.

The trustee must use the property only for the beneficiary. The trust instrument usually explains (sometimes in detail, sometimes very generally) how the donor intended the trustee to use the property for the beneficiary. Often the trustee is given *discretion* to make specific decisions as to how to use the trust funds. This Manual tells the trustees how to use that discretion in managing a Special Needs Trust.

Some trusts can be *revocable*. That is, they can be amended (changed) or revoked by the grantor. Other trusts are *irrevocable*. In that case, they cannot be revoked (except in some cases by a court order) or modified by the grantor. Some irrevocable trusts, however, including many Special Needs Trusts, can be modified by the trustee (but not the grantor) in order to remain in compliance with relevant federal or state laws.

What is the purpose of a Special (or Supplemental) Needs Trust?

A Special Needs Trust is established to supplement but not replace the benefits a disabled beneficiary receives from SSI, Medicaid, and other government benefit programs. Individuals with disabilities, particularly those who are unable to be gainfully employed due to their disabilities, often receive government assistance to help them maintain themselves in the community. The most common of these programs are Supplemental Security Income (SSI) and Medicaid. Both SSI and Medicaid are modeled on welfare programs and usually require a person to be impoverished in order to receive benefits. If an individual has too many assets or too much income, then he will not qualify for SSI benefits even if he is disabled. In many states, he will also be ineligible for Medicaid. However, a person can have a Special Needs Trust and still qualify for these programs.

Special Needs Trusts are commonly used in estate planning because parents of children with disabilities are often faced with a dilemma: If they leave assets directly to their child with disabilities, he or she will not qualify for most government benefit programs. However, disinheriting the child is not necessary or recommended. A Special Needs Trust can allow a person with disabilities to receive government benefits and still have a source of funds to pay for extras that government programs do not provide. In this way, these trusts can enhance the quality of life for a person with a disability.

Also, a person with a disability can fund a Special Needs Trust for himself or herself. The trust can hold the person's money, such as financial compensation from an injury or a retroactive award of disability benefits. These self-settled trusts are discussed later in this chapter.

How does a Special Needs Trust Operate?

The trustee must use the funds in a manner that considers the beneficiary's entitlement to SSI, Medicaid, and other public benefit programs. All of these programs have rigorous and complicated rules about how distributions from a Special Needs Trust may affect a person's eligibility for public benefits.

For example, the assets in a properly drafted Special Needs Trust are considered "non-countable assets" for purposes of SSI eligibility. This means that the mere existence of a Special Needs Trust will not disqualify a person from receiving SSI. However, if the trustee makes any cash payments directly to the beneficiary, those payments may be considered income to the beneficiary. This income can potentially reduce or eliminate the person's SSI benefit. Also, if the trustee makes any payments from the trust for food or shelter items, those payments are considered "in-kind" income. This in-kind income can also reduce the person's SSI benefits. Thus, in most cases, the trustee should be careful not to distribute any money in a way that will cause a problem with SSI. However, some Special Needs Trusts allow the trustee to distribute money even if it affects the person's public benefits. For example, a trustee might purchase suitable housing for the beneficiary even if it reduces his SSI stipend. This might be necessary if the beneficiary's need for housing exceeds the value of the government benefit.

Are there Different Kinds of Special Needs Trusts?

Yes. There are two basic kinds of Special Needs Trusts: self-settled trusts and third party trusts.

A *self-settled trust* is funded with the disabled beneficiary's own assets. (A self-settled trust is sometimes called a first party trust.) For example, a person with a disability who receives a personal injury settlement might put the proceeds into a self-settled trust for his own use. A self-settled trust could also be funded with savings, inherited money, or a retroactive award of disability benefits. If a person places assets in a self-settled trust in order to obtain SSI, then the trust must meet certain requirements. For one thing, it must be irrevocable. Also, due to a wrinkle in the law, the trust must be created by a parent, grandparent, legal guardian, or a court. In other words, a person cannot create a self-settled trust for himself. Also, the trust must contain a so-called Medicaid "payback" provision (see discussion below).

A *third party trust* is one that contains assets that belonged to someone other than the disabled beneficiary before they were put in the trust. A classic example of a third party trust is one that a parent creates in order to leave an inheritance to a disabled child. A parent can create a third party trust under his or her will, through a separate Special Needs Trust document, or through a living trust. In most cases, a third party trust will not contain any funds until the parent dies. However, some parents may put assets in a third party trust while they are alive in order to qualify for Medicaid benefits for themselves (see discussion below).

When the Disabled Beneficiary Dies, do the Remaining Trust Funds go to the State?

Not necessarily. In general, what will happen to any remaining funds depends on whether the trust is a self-settled trust or a third party trust.

In most cases, any funds that remain in a *self-settled trust* when the disabled beneficiary dies must be used to repay the state for any Medicaid benefits the beneficiary received while he was alive. This is necessary because self-settled trusts are subject to special rules under the SSI and Medicaid programs. The most important of these rules is that if the beneficiary wants to receive SSI, the trust must contain a so-called Medicaid payback provision. That provision states that when the disabled beneficiary dies, the state must be repaid for the Medicaid benefits it provided to the beneficiary. (However, any funds that remain after the state has been paid can go to other people who have been named in the trust. These "remainder beneficiaries" are usually the disabled beneficiary's family members.) What if the trust does not contain such a Medicaid payback provision? Then it will probably be considered a countable asset under the SSI rules. This means that the beneficiary cannot get SSI. (However, self-settled trusts that were created before January 1, 2000 do not need Medicaid payback language.) Obviously these rules create a strong incentive to include a payback provision in any self-settled Special Needs Trust.

By contrast, any funds that remain in a *third party trust* do not go to the state. Instead, the funds can usually pass to the remainder beneficiaries.

In a few cases, however, a third party trust must provide for government reimbursement. A classic example involves an elderly parent who needs nursing home care but has too many assets to qualify for Medicaid long term care benefits. The parent can transfer his or her assets to a Special Needs Trust for a disabled child and qualify for benefits right away. (This is an exception to the rule that imposes a waiting period of up to 5 years to receive Medicaid benefits if a person transfers assets to a trust.) In this limited situation, the Special Needs Trust must contain a payback provision. That provision must state that when the beneficiary (the disabled child) dies, the state will be reimbursed for the child's (not the parent's) lifetime medical benefits.

However, we emphasize that this situation is the exception rather than the rule. *In most cases, a third party Special Needs Trust does not need to pay back the state. Thus, when the disabled beneficiary dies, any funds that are left in the trust can usually pass to other family members.*

Is There any Difference between a Special Needs Trust and a Supplemental Needs Trust?

In this book, we do not distinguish between a Special Needs Trust and a Supplemental Needs Trust. We are aware that in Massachusetts, some advisors use the term "Supplemental Needs Trust" to mean a third party trust (such as a trust that a parent creates for his or her disabled child). Also, the usage may be different in different states. However, in our experience, most people (both attorneys and non-attorneys) use the terms interchangeably. We think there is no harm in doing so. Thus, in this book, we use both terms to mean the same thing.

CHAPTER 2

PUBLIC BENEFIT PROGRAMS

What public benefit programs does the Trustee need to understand?

There are several basic public benefit programs for people with disabilities that the Trustee should understand. The four major programs are Supplemental Security Income (SSI), Social Security Disability Income (SSDI), Medicaid (called MassHealth in Massachusetts) and Medicare. Also, trustees of trusts for minor (under age 18) beneficiaries should be familiar with the Transitional Aid to Families With Dependent Children program (TAFDC) and, in Massachusetts, the Kaleigh Mulligan program. The eligibility requirements and other pertinent information about these programs are described below.

Supplemental Security Income (SSI)

SSI, a federal benefit program, pays monthly cash benefits to aged, blind, or disabled individuals who have limited income and financial resources. The SSI program is funded from the general revenues of the U.S. Treasury and is administered by the Social Security Administration (SSA). SSI benefits are sometimes called Title XVI benefits.

In Massachusetts, SSI recipients automatically receive MassHealth.

How does one qualify for SSI?

To become eligible for SSI, one must:
- Have limited income and few resources; and

6

- Be aged, medically disabled, or blind according to the Social Security's definition; and
- Initially, be not working, or working but earning less than $830 per month (in 2005) and
- Be a U.S. citizen or meet alien status criteria.

How does the SSI program define disability?

Disability for adults is defined as the inability to engage in "substantial gainful activity" (SGA). There must be a physical or mental impairment, or combination of impairments, that can be expected to last for a continuous period of at least 12 months, or result in death. 20 C.F.R. § 416.905.

The Social Security Administration has established certain earnings levels as reasonable signs that a person can perform SGA. For the year 2005, that level is $830 per month a non-blind person, and $1,380 for a blind person. If one can potentially earn $830 or more (or $1,380 or more if blind), then Social Security presumes that that person is able to engage in SGA. The presumed SGA amount is indexed to an annual cost of living allowance and is adjusted in January of each year.

How much does SSI pay?

The amount of SSI one may receive (the "Maximum Benefit Rate" or "maximum SSI benefit amount") depends on three factors:

1. The recipient's living arrangement; and
2. Whether the recipient is married; and
3. Whether the recipient is elderly, disabled, or blind.

Some states, including Massachusetts, supplement the federal SSI benefit. Massachusetts recipients get both a federal benefit and a state supplement in one monthly check.

In 2005, in Massachusetts, the lowest SSI benefit amount is $490.36. That is for a single, non-blind disabled person, under age 65, who lives in another person's household. The highest benefit amount is $1,033. That is for an aged (65 or older) or blind disabled person in assisted living.

The table of Maximum Benefit Rates for all categories in Massachusetts for the year 2005 can be found in the Appendix.

How many resources can a person have and receive SSI?

The SSI rules distinguish between *countable* and *non-countable* resources. Countable resource limits are $2,000 for an individual and $3,000 for a couple.

A countable resource is generally defined as cash or other liquid asset or real property that the applicant owns and could convert to cash. 20 C.F.R. § 416.1201.

Examples of countable resources are:
- Cash, which is not the current month's income;
- Income producing property, including real estate;
- Stocks, bonds, investments;
- Life insurance with a cash value in excess of $1,500;

20 C.F.R.§ 416.1201.

Examples of non-countable resources are:
- Personal residence (home, including a condominium);
- Automobiles of any value;
- Assets in a Plan for Achieving Self-Support (PASS);
- Burial insurance;
- Life insurance with a cash value of less than $1,500.

20 C.F.R.§ 416.1210.

How much income can an applicant have?

One's countable income must be below the maximum SSI benefit amount established for his particular benefit category. As explained earlier, one's maximum benefit amount depends on his living arrangement, whether he is married, and his type of disability (i.e., blind or non-blind). The SSI payment may be reduced depending on how much, and what kind of, income the individual receives.

What is income?

Under SSI rules, income can be *earned, unearned,* or *in-kind.*

What is unearned income?

Unearned income is income that is not received from work. Unearned income includes periodic payments, such as Social Security benefits, annuities, alimony, child support, dividends, interest from bank accounts, royalties, and rents, and one-time benefits such as prizes, awards, gifts, and inheritances. Distributions of cash from a Special Needs Trust are unearned income. 20 C.F.R. §§ 416.1120; 416.1121.

How does unearned income affect SSI?

An SSI recipient may receive up to $20 per month of unearned income without penalty. Any unearned income in excess of $20 per month will be deducted from the SSI benefit on a dollar-for-dollar basis.

For example, John lives independently and has unearned income of $500.00 per month from an annuity.

$500.00   unearned income
-$20.00   SSI General Exclusion
$480.00   total countable unearned income

Thus, John would receive

$693.39   maximum SSI benefit amount (in 2005)
-$480.00   total countable unearned income
$213.39   reduced SSI benefit

What is earned income?

Earned income is earnings from wages or self-employment. Payment for work performed in a sheltered workshop is included within the definition of earned income. C.F.R. § 416.1110.

How does earned income affect SSI?

The receipt of earned income over $65 per month (or $85 per month if there is no unearned income) will reduce the SSI benefit. The formula to calculate the SSI benefit if there is earned income, is as follows:

1. Deduct the SSI General Exclusion of $20 (if not used up on unearned income), then
2. Deduct $65 per month (the SSI Earned Income Exclusion), then
3. Deduct one-half of the remaining earned income.

The balance is total countable earned income.

Then the total amount of countable earned income is deducted from the maximum SSI benefit amount. The remaining balance is the reduced SSI benefit.

For example, John lives independently, earns $150 per month from a part-time job, and has no unearned income.

$150.00	earned income
-$20.00	SSI General Exclusion
$130.00	
-$65.00	SSI Earned Income Exclusion
$65.00	
-$32.50	one-half of remaining earned income
$32.50	total countable earned income

Thus, John would receive:

$693.39	maximum SSI benefit amount (in 2005)
-$32.50	total countable earned income
$660.89	reduced SSI benefit

What is in-kind income?

Under the pertinent Social Security regulations, an SSI recipient is expected to pay for all of his food and shelter costs out of his SSI stipend. Often this is quite difficult, so sometimes an SSI recipient must get assistance from relatives or others to pay for his basic living expenses. However, if an SSI recipient receives food or shelter from a third party, then according to Social Security rules, he has received "in-kind income" and his benefit may be reduced. Social Security rules define in-kind income as "not cash, but food or shelter, or something the recipient can use to get one of those three items." Ref. 20 C.F.R.§§ 416.1102; 416.1130. Another term for in-kind income is "in-kind support and maintenance" (ISM).

How does in-kind support and maintenance affect SSI?

Receipt of any in-kind support and maintenance may reduce SSI benefits. Social Security has two ways to calculate this type of income depending on the individual's particular circumstances: the One-Third Reduction Rule and the Presumed Maximum Value Rule.

The One-Third Reduction Rule. This rule is used only in one limited situation, which is when the SSI recipient lives for a full calendar month in the household of another person who provides both food and shelter to him without charge. When the One-Third Reduction Rule is used, the SSI benefit amount is reduced by one-third of the federal benefit amount. 20 C.F.R. § 416.1131; POMS SI 00835.200.

> For example, John, age 50, lives with his sister and her husband who provide him with both food and shelter. John's SSI monthly benefit will be reduced by one-third of the federal benefit rate for his category.

The Presumed Maximum Value Rule. Social Security uses this rule when an SSI recipient has received food or shelter from an outside source, and the One Third Reduction Rule does not apply. For instance, if in the above example, John did not receive *both* food and shelter from his sister, or if he lived in his own home and got outside help with living expenses, then the One-Third Reduction Rule would not apply because John has not received both food and shelter in another person's household. Instead, in that situation, Social Security would use the Presumed Maximum Value Rule (PMV). Under that rule, rather than determine the *actual* value of any food or shelter item, Social Security *presumes* that the item has a maximum value, which is the one-third of the federal benefit amount, plus $20. Since the federal benefit in 2005 is $579 per month, the SSI benefit is reduced by $213 ($579 x 1/3 + $20)[1]. 20 C.F.R.§ 1140; POMS SI 00835.300. Note that only the federal benefit—not the state supplement—is reduced.

> For example, John lives in Massachusetts in an apartment owned by his brother. The market rate is $750, but John pays only $500. John's maximum SSI benefit amount is $693.39 ($579 federal + $114.39 state). The actual value of the reduced rent is $250, but the presumed value of the reduced rent is only $213 ($579 x 1/3 + $20), so John has total countable in-kind income of $213.

> Thus, John would receive:

> $693.39   maximum SSI benefit amount (in 2005)
> -$213.00   total countable in-kind income
> $480.39   reduced SSI benefit

The SSI recipient may attempt to prove that the *actual* current market value of the item received is *less* than the *presumed* value assigned by Social Security. If he succeeds in so persuading Social Security, then the item's actual value will be used.

> For example, John's parents pay his gas and electric bills, which total $75. John's SSI is reduced by only $75.

Fortunately, regardless of the amount of in-kind support and maintenance, the SSI benefit is never reduced by more than one-third of the federal benefit, plus $20. Thus, in the above example, even if the fair market rental of John's apartment were $1,000, the maximum deduction would not exceed $213.

Another important point is that Social Security does not apply both the One-Third Reduction Rule and the Presumed Maximum Value Rule to a recipient in any one month. In other words, if Social Security pays a reduced SSI benefit under the One-Third Reduction Rule, then any additional in-kind income is

---

1. Some SSI recipients are married to other SSI recipients (SSI couples). The federal benefit rate for each such individual is $434.50. Thus, the presumed maximum value would be $164.83 ($434.50 x 1/3 +$20).

disregarded, regardless of the amount. 20 C.F.R. §416.1131(b); POMS SI 00835.001A.

> For example, John lives independently and his family pays his rent one month. His SSI check is reduced by one-third for that month. In the same month, his parents buy him $100 worth of groceries. John's SSI check will not be reduced again even though he received in-kind income (food).

Finally, it is important to note that bills paid by a third party directly to a vendor (seller or supplier) for items that are *not* food or shelter do *not* result in countable income to the SSI recipient. 20 C.F.R. § 416.1103(g).

Can children get SSI?

Blind or disabled children can qualify for SSI. However, in addition to the income and asset counting rules described above, other special financial eligibility rules apply. Until the child reaches age 18, a portion of the income and assets of parents who live with the child may be attributed ("deemed") to the child for eligibility purposes. For asset deeming purposes, there are certain asset limits for both the child and the deemor parent or parents. For example, the asset limit for a child in a two-parent household is $5,000, and that of a child in a one-parent household is $4,000. Because of these restrictive deeming rules, many children with disabilities cannot get SSI until their eighteenth birthdays, when they can qualify under the adult rules.

There are different disability rules for children as well as different financial rules. Since a work test does not make sense for children, Social Security looks for a mental or physical impairment, or combination of impairments, that substantially affects the child's ability to reach age appropriate developmental milestones, or to engage in age appropriate activities of daily living. Essentially, Social Security compares the functioning of SSI applicant children to that of same age children without disabilities. 20 C.F.R § 416.924

Can a person have a Special Needs Trust and get SSI?

Yes. Resources held in a Special Needs Trust do not count as the resources of an SSI recipient. To qualify, the trust can either have been created by another person, such as the beneficiary's parent ("third party trust"), or by the disabled beneficiary himself ("self-settled trust"). In each case, the trust must be irrevocable, and the beneficiary can only have very limited, if any, control over how the trust assets are used.

There are special rules for trusts established on or after January 1, 2000, that contain the assets of a person who receives SSI. In that case, the trust must have been created by the beneficiary's parent, grandparent, guardian, or a court; be for the sole benefit of the beneficiary; and provide that upon the beneficiary's death, the state will be reimbursed for all Medicaid benefits that the beneficiary received. Since the law governing these trusts is relatively new, it is especially important for the trustee who is administering one to work with a qualified attorney.

Do distributions from a Special Needs Trust affect SSI?

Trust distributions could affect the benefit amount depending on the form and amount of the distribution. As explained earlier in this section, cash distributions in excess of $20 per month will be counted as unearned income and reduce the SSI benefit on a dollar-for-dollar basis. If the trust regularly pays for food or shelter, then these kinds of distributions will be counted as in-kind support and maintenance. The SSI benefit will be reduced by the actual value of the item supplied, or one-third of the federal benefit amount, plus $20, whichever is less. In-kind distributions for items other than food and shelter are *not income* and do not affect the SSI benefit. 20 C.F.R. §416.1103(g).

Social Security Disability Insurance (SSDI)

SSDI, a federal program, pays monthly cash benefits to disabled workers (and their dependents) who have paid Social Security taxes on their earnings. SSDI is funded by FICA withholdings on wages and by taxes on self-employment income. SSDI is administered by the Social Security Administration.

SSDI benefits are sometimes called Title II benefits. SSDI is also known as Retirement, Survivors, and Disability Insurance ("RSDI").

Unlike SSI, financial eligibility for SSDI is *not* based on economic need. Instead, financial eligibility is based on one's earnings record.

An important benefit of the SSDI program is that *SSDI recipients qualify for Medicare (but not Medicaid) after receiving SSDI benefits for 24 months.*

How does one qualify for SSDI?

To qualify for SSDI, an individual must:

1. Have sufficient quarters of covered employment; and

2. Be medically disabled; and

3. Be not working, or if working, earning less than $830 per month (in 2005); or

4. Be the minor (under age 18) child of a retired, disabled or deceased worker; or

5. Be the widow(er) of a deceased worker; or

6. Be the disabled adult child (whose disability began before age 22) of a parent covered by Social Security who retires, becomes disabled, or dies.

How much does SSDI pay?

One's SSDI benefit depends on his (or his parent's) primary insurance amount (PIA). A worker's PIA is established by Social Security according to a complicated formula that includes the number of years worked, the maximum Social Security wage base during those years, and the worker's actual wages or self-employment income.

In addition to the PIA, Social Security establishes a "Family Maximum Benefit" for each insured worker. The Family Maximum Benefit places a limit on the total amount of benefits that Social Security must pay based on the worker's earnings record. That is, if a retired, deceased, or disabled worker has dependent family members, then the total benefits payable to the worker and/or his family may not exceed the Family Maximum Benefit set by Social Security. However, the worker's benefit is paid first and is not affected by any dependents' benefits on his or her record. 20 C.F.R. § 404.403.

The disabled adult son or daughter[2] of a disabled, retired, or deceased worker may qualify for SSDI benefits based on his or her parent's earnings record. To obtain SSDI benefits, these children must have been disabled before age 22.

A disabled adult son or daughter's SSDI benefit is equal to 50 percent of the parent's PIA while the worker is living and 75 percent of the PIA after the parent has died. But, as noted above, in some situations the SSDI benefit may be subject to the Family Maximum Benefit and, therefore, the benefit may be reduced. 20 C.F.R.§ 404.353.

Can one receive both SSI and SSDI?

Yes. An SSDI recipient who receives a low monthly benefit can also get SSI. Those who get both SSI and SSDI are called "dual recipients." The combined benefits raise the disabled person's income to the maximum SSI benefit amount for his category.

> For example, John receives SSDI of $450 per month based on his deceased father's earnings. The maximum SSI benefit based on John's living situation is $609.40 per month. John receives SSI of $149.40 per month to raise his total public benefits to the maximum SSI amount for his category.

In some states, dual recipients may receive both Medicare, based on SSDI status, and Medicaid, based on SSI entitlement.

How does the SSDI program define disability?

The SSDI program's definition of disability is the same one used in the SSI program for adults, namely, "the inability to engage in substantial gainful activity because of a medically determined impairment or combination of impairments that can be expected to result in death or to last for a continuous period of not less than 12 months." 404 C.F.R. § 1505.

---

2. Also called a disabled adult child (DAC)

In 2005, Social Security presumes that if a person can earn $830 or more per month ($1,380 if blind), then that person is able to engage in SGA and, therefore, is not disabled. (See discussion of SGA in the SSI portion of this section.)

SSDI benefits for disabled workers begin after they have been eligible for disability benefits for at least five months.

How many assets can a person have and receive SSDI?

Unlike SSI, there are no asset limits for the SSDI program.

Do unearned and in-kind income affect SSDI?

No. Unlike SSI, SSDI has no limits on unearned income or in-kind income.

Does earned income affect SSDI?

In 2005, Social Security assumes that if a person can earn $830 or more per month, then that person is able to engage in SGA and is, therefore, not disabled. But, some recipients who use certain "work incentives" can earn more than the SGA limit for certain periods of time. This is discussed in the Work Incentives section of this manual.

Can a person have a Special Needs Trust and get SSDI?

Yes. Since there are no financial criteria for SSDI (other than the earnings test for SGA), a Special Needs Trust will not affect eligibility.

Medicare

Medicare, a federal health insurance program, is administered by the Centers for Medicare & Medicaid Services (CMS, formerly HCFA), through private health insurance companies.

How does a person qualify for Medicare?

To qualify for Medicare, a person must:

1. Be 65 years of age or older; and

2. Be a U.S. citizen, a permanent resident, or a resident alien who has been in the U.S. for at least 5 years; and

3. Have worked for at least 10 years in Medicare covered employment (or be the spouse of one who has); or

4. Be a younger person with a disability; or

5. Have end-stage kidney disease; or

6. Be the disabled child (whose disability began before age 22) of a Medicare recipient.

Individuals with disabilities who qualify for SSDI, based either on their own prior work history or a disabled or deceased parent's benefits, may receive Medicare coverage from the federal government after they have qualified for SSDI for 24 months.

What does Medicare pay for?

Medicare is divided into three parts: Medicare A, B, and C.

Medicare A (hospital insurance) covers hospital stays and related care, some home health services, care in a skilled nursing facility, and hospice care.

Medicare B (medical insurance) covers hospital outpatient services, physician visits, ambulance transportation, and some home health care.

Medicare C (Medicare + Choice) allows beneficiaries to receive services in alternative ways, such as certain Health Maintenance Organizations (HMO's), Preferred Provider Organizations (PPO's), and Point of Service Plans (POS's).

How much does Medicare cost?

For most recipients, Medicare A is free (except for the annual deductible described below). The premium for Medicare B is $78.20 per month in 2005, which sum is automatically deducted from the Social Security benefit check. In some states, including Massachusetts, Medicare recipients with very low income and few assets can qualify for state assistance in paying the Medicare B premium.

Are there any deductibles or payments?

Yes. In 2005, the deductible for Medicare A is $912 per benefit period. Medicare B has an annual deductible of $110. Medicare pays for 80 percent of covered charges and the patient pays 20 percent. In Massachusetts, some Medicare recipients with very low income and few assets can qualify for state assistance to pay the amounts Medicare does not pay.

Are there are any income or asset limits?

No. There are no financial restrictions for Medicare.

What is Medigap Insurance?

Some persons who receive Medicare purchase supplemental medical insurance, called Medigap insurance, to cover the amounts that Medicare does not pay. In Massachusetts, the most common Medigap program is Medex (offered by Blue Cross and Blue Shield). Medigap coverage pays the 20 percent balance not covered by Medicare.

Medicaid and Related Medical Programs in Massachusetts

Medicaid, a federal- and state-funded health insurance program, provides medical benefits for low- and middle-income individuals (and their families) and for disabled individuals. In Massachusetts, the Medicaid program (called MassHealth) is administered by the Division of Medical Assistance (DMA).

Although Medicaid is a federally funded program, the federal government in some instances has given the states leeway to adopt their own rules. As a result, the Medicaid financial eligibility rules and benefits are different in each state. This section explains the Medicaid rules in Massachusetts. Trustees in other states should consult with a local attorney for guidance in this area.

How does one qualify for Medicaid, and what does Medicaid pay for?

In Massachusetts, there are different MassHealth coverage types and different eligibility rules depending on one's age (65 and older, or under 65) and whether one lives in an institution or in the community.[3] The following describes some of the pertinent coverage types and financial rules for each group. Note that the DMA adjusts its figures for premium costs on April 1 of each year.

Institutionalized individuals: People with disabilities of any age who reside in institutions such as nursing homes, rehab facilities, or state hospitals can receive MassHealth long-term care benefits that pay for all of their room and board, nursing care, and medical costs that are not covered by other medical insurance. To qualify for these long term care benefits, one can own no more than $2,000 in countable assets. If a person gives away property to reduce his assets to the $2,000 limit, then there may be a waiting period of up to 36 months (five years for trusts), depending on the amount transferred, before benefits can be obtained.

In general, institutionalized individuals must pay all of their income to the institution, except for $60 that they are allowed to retain, before MassHealth will provide benefits. If an institutionalized person has less than $60 in monthly personal income, then the Commonwealth will pay that person up to $60 per month as a personal needs allowance. 130 C.M.R. § 520.026(A)(2).

It is important to note that people with disabilities who live in institutions cannot get SSI. 20 C.F.R.§ 416.211. Thus, an SSI recipient who enters an institution will lose SSI and MassHealth (community benefits) and must qualify for MassHealth under the long term care rules, which are different from the community rules.

Community residents: People with disabilities who reside in community settings such as apartments, private homes, and state funded group homes for people with mental illness or mental retardation ("community residents") may receive MassHealth community benefits. There are currently seven different

---

3. The rules for persons under age 65 who live in the community are located at 130 C.M.R.§§ 501.000–508.018. The rules for individuals age 65 and older, and institutionalized individuals of any age, are located at 130 C.M.R.§§ 515.000–523.041.

coverage types that pay for a range of services. For some programs, there are different rules depending on whether one is over or under age 65.

A description of the seven MassHealth coverage types is contained in the MassHealth Member Booklet, which can be obtained from the DMA. (See the "Where to Go for Help" section of this manual.) The most important MassHealth programs for community residents are MassHealth Standard and CommonHealth. Also, Prescription Advantage may pay for prescription drugs for people not covered by MassHealth Standard. The pertinent rules of those three programs are summarized below.

A. *MassHealth* Standard: 130 C.M.R. §502. The most generous program is MassHealth Standard, which pays for 100 percent of most medical and related services, including hospital care, outpatient services, durable medical equipment, doctor visits, mental health services, prescription medications, and some limited dental care. For adults with disabilities, MassHealth Standard pays for most day programs, transportation, and residential care. For adults with disabilities who also get Medicare Part B, MassHealth Standard will pay for the Medicare premium, co-insurance, and deductibles.

Currently in Massachusetts, most MassHealth Standard recipients under age 65 must enroll in a managed care plan.

SSI recipients automatically receive MassHealth Standard, so recipients are understandably concerned about what happens to Medicaid if they lose SSI. In Massachusetts, when SSI ends, MassHealth is extended while the Division explores whether the individual may be eligible for any other MassHealth programs. 130 CMR § 505.002(F(1). Also, individuals who lose SSI solely because they now qualify for SSDI based on their parents' earnings will automatically continue to receive Medicaid.[4] 130 C.M.R. §§ 505.002(F)(2)(b), 519.004.

Also, it is possible for a person with a disability to qualify for MassHealth Standard based solely on his income, independent of SSI. However, there are different eligibility rules depending whether one is age 65 or over, or under 65.

---

4. A typical situation involves an SSI recipient whose parent has retired or died. When that person begins to receive SSDI based on his parent's work record, he may lose SSI because he has too much income. However, Medicaid will continue even if his income from SSDI might otherwise be too high for Medicaid.

Individuals under age 65 (in 2005) must have gross monthly income from all sources of no more than $1,063 for a single individual, or $1,425 for a couple (i.e. 133% of the Federal Poverty Level in 2005). There is currently no asset limit for those under age 65. 130 C.M.R. § 505.002(F). However, the DMA has recently proposed regulations that would impose asset limits on MassHealth applicants under age 65. The new rules regarding asset limits have not been implemented at the time this manual is printed.

Individuals age 65 and over, in 2005, by contrast to those under age 65, may retain no more than $2,000 in countable assets ($3,000 for a couple). The income limit is 100 percent of the Federal Poverty Level, which is $798.00 for a single individual, or $1,069 for a couple in 2005. If one's income exceeds those limits, then he may qualify for MassHealth by meeting a deductible every six months. That deductible is met when incurred medical costs not covered by other health insurance meet or exceed a standard set by the state. 130 C.M.R. §§ 520.030, 519.005(A)(1). A sample computation of the deductible is provided in the MassHealth booklet (see the "Where To Go For Help" Section).

B. *CommonHealth*. 130 C.M.R. § 505.004. CommonHealth medical benefits are almost identical to those of MassHealth Standard. However, there are differences in the financial rules for the two programs. CommonHealth members must pay a monthly premium that is set on a sliding scale according to one's family composition and annual family income. Also, some CommonHealth members must meet a one-time deductible (described below).

In 2003, the DMA imposed a limit on the amount of assets a person can own and still receive CommonHealth. However, this limit has not been implemented at the time of this printing (August, 2005).

Disabled children under age 18 who are not eligible for MassHealth Standard can qualify for CommonHealth by paying a premium that is based on a sliding scale according to family income. 130 C.M.R.§ 505.004(D).

Disabled 18 year olds can qualify whether or not they are working, as long as they are permanently and totally disabled according to the DMA definition. 130 C.M.R.§ 505.004(E).

Disabled working adults age 19 through 64 can qualify by paying a premium. "Working" is defined as being employed an average of 40 hours or more per month, or if employed less than 40 hours per month, having worked 240 hours in the six months preceding application for benefits. 130 C.M.R.§ 505.004(B).

Non-working disabled adults age 19 through 64 who do not qualify for MassHealth Standard may qualify for CommonHealth by meeting a one-time deductible. 130 C.M.R.§ 505.004(C). That deductible is the amount by which family income exceeds an amount set by the Division. The Division of Medical Assistance offers the following example of the one-time deductible (from the MassHealth Member Booklet):

A family of two persons has monthly income, before taxes and after permissible deductible expenses, of $1,327. Thus,

$1,327
-$670   income standard for family of two
$657   excess income
x 6   six-month deductible period
$3,942   deductible amount

In this example, in order to qualify for CommonHealth, the family must incur medical bills of $3,942 that are not covered by any other medical insurance. The medical bills must be incurred within the six month period specified by MassHealth.

Disabled working adults age 65 and older can qualify by paying a premium. The definition of "working" is the same as for those under age 65. There is no asset limit for this category. 130 C.M.R. § 519.012.

One can purchase either full or supplemental CommonHealth insurance. Full coverage pays for all services for the individual who has no other health insurance. Supplemental coverage pays for services and items not covered by the individual's primary insurance.

C. _Prescription Advantage:_ Prescription Advantage, also called The Pharmacy Program, pays for prescription drugs for elderly and certain disabled individuals, up to $1,250 per year (July 1–June 30). The Pharmacy Program rules are located at 130 CMR § 523.000. Also, information about the current eligibility rules, premium amounts, and so forth, is available by calling 1-800-AGE-INFO, or from The Pharmacy Program website (www.800ageinfo.com).

Disabled individuals under age 65 who do not receive MassHealth or CommonHealth may qualify if their income is less than $17,503 for a single person ($23,481 for a couple), and they are not working, or if working, are employed less than 40 hours per month.

Any disabled or non-disabled person age 65 and over may qualify by paying a monthly premium that ranges from $0 (for a single person with annual income of $12,596 or less), to $99 (for a single person with annual income of $46,551 or more).

Once enrolled, there is a nominal annual enrollment fee of $15. There may also be a monthly premium and an annual deductible. Once the deductible has been met, there is a co-payment, according to one's income, for prescription drugs (currently $9 to $12 for generic drugs; $23 to $30 for some brand-name drugs, and $45 to $50 for certain other brand-name drugs). However, the maximum out-of-pocket expenses (excluding premiums) will not exceed $2,000 or 10 percent of household gross annual income for a single person or a couple with only one spouse in the plan ($3,000 or 10 percent of income for a married couple with both spouses in the plan).

How does a Special Needs Trust affect eligibility for MassHealth?

For _community residents under age 65_, the existence of a properly drafted Special Needs Trust should not affect eligibility for MassHealth programs. Also, since there are currently no asset restrictions for that program, one may transfer assets to a Special Needs Trust without penalty. However, if the trustee makes any cash distributions from the trust directly to a MassHealth recipient, then those distributions will be counted as income which may affect eligibility, since one can have only limited income to qualify. However, if the trustee makes distributions to third parties for payment of goods and services provided to a MassHealth recipient, then those distributions will not affect eligibility. This is true even if the distributions are for food and shelter, because unlike SSI, the MassHealth program does not count such "in-kind" income. 130 C.M.R. § 506.004.

Institutionalized persons of any age and community residents age 65 and over can benefit from a Special Needs Trust and still qualify for MassHealth benefits. Unlike community residents under age 65, these individuals may own no more than $2,000 in resources, so a Special Needs Trust may be especially helpful. However, if a recipient transfers his own assets to a Special Needs Trust in order to reach the $2,000 asset limit, then a disqualification period may be imposed.[5] If the trustee makes cash distributions from the trust directly to a recipient, then those distributions will be counted as income, which may affect financial eligibility. However, if the trustee makes any distributions to third parties who provide goods and services to a recipient, then those distributions will not affect eligibility, even if they are for food or shelter, because the MassHealth program does not count this "in-kind" income.

Transitional Aid to Families With Dependent Children (TAFDC)

TAFDC, a federal benefit program, pays cash benefits to certain needy children who are deprived of parental support. TAFDC can be an important financial resource for children with disabilities. In Massachusetts, TAFDC is administered by the Department of Transitional Assistance (DTA) (formerly the Department of Public Welfare).

TAFDC recipients automatically receive Medicaid.

How does one qualify for TAFDC?

To qualify for TAFDC, there must be both a "needy" child and a caretaker relative of that child in the household. The child must be deprived of support from

---

5. One exception is if the resources are transferred to a Special Needs Trust for a disabled person (other than the MassHealth recipient) *and* the trust contains a so-called Medicaid payback provision. (A Medicaid payback provision states that when the beneficiary dies, the remaining trust assets must be used to reimburse the state for the beneficiary's Medicaid services.)

at least one parent because that parent is deceased, absent from the home, physically or mentally unable to care for the child, or unemployed or underemployed according to strict regulations enacted by the Commonwealth.

There are stringent asset and income tests for the household (called the "filing unit"). The household may not have more than $2,500 in countable assets. Also, the household's income may not exceed the limits established by the Commonwealth under complicated income counting rules. 106 C.M.R. §204.100.

Can a person have a Special Needs Trust and receive TAFCD?

Yes. The existence of a properly drafted Special Needs Trust will not affect one's eligibility for TAFDC. These trust funds are considered "inaccessible assets" under program rules. 106 CMR §204.125. Also, irrevocable trusts that contain up to $150,000 of assets derived from a child's personal injury award or settlement are not counted.

However, there are important limitations on who may act as trustee. The trustee may *not* be an individual who is under the direction or control of any household member who receives TAFDC. Therefore, if TAFDC benefits are needed, the parent should not act as trustee of a child's Special Needs Trust. An independent or professional trustee should be employed.

How do distributions from a Special Needs Trust affect TAFDC?

Distributions for food or shelter are considered in-kind income that may reduce the monthly benefit.

However, distributions from a Special Needs Trust that holds the disabled child's personal injury award or settlement will not be counted if the distributions are used to meet the child's special needs which result from the injury, such as rehabilitative therapies, pain management, personal care attendants, education-related expenses, vocational training or rehabilitation; transportation related needs such as the purchase and/or retrofitting of a van; and special equipment, clothing, or services for the disabled child. But, items such as vacations, recreational equipment (including a swimming pool), or leisure activities would presumptively *not* be for the child's special needs and could cause a problem with TAFDC. 106 C.M.R. §2404.240(B)(5).

The Kaleigh Mulligan Program

In Massachusetts, the Kaleigh Mulligan Program provides a Medicaid institutional level of benefits for children with severe disabilities who are under age 18, if such benefits are required for the child to remain at home instead of being placed in a pediatric nursing home or other institutional setting.

The parents' income and assets are disregarded for financial eligibility purposes. The child must have very limited income and $2,000 or less in countable assets in his own name. 130 C.M.R. § 519.007(A)(1). A properly drafted Special Needs Trust is not a countable asset.

Also, the child must need skilled nursing facility or hospital-level care and be permanently and totally disabled, as defined by SSI criteria. 130 C.M.R. § 519.007(A)(1)(a). 130 C.M.R. 519.007A

CHAPTER 3

HOUSING

Finding decent, affordable housing can be especially challenging for low-income people with disabilities. Yet, despite the odds, many people with disabilities live independently in apartments, and some even own their own homes. In this section we discuss what housing costs the trustee may safely pay from trust funds and which ones she should not pay. We also discuss the section 8 housing subsidy program and explain how the Special Needs Trust may affect that program.

How does payment of housing costs by a Special Needs Trust affect SSI?

In most states, including Massachusetts, an SSI recipient is expected to pay for all of his housing expenses out of his SSI stipend. If he receives outside assistance with housing costs of more than $20 per month, then his SSI benefit will be reduced.[6] Fortunately, not every housing related item causes a problem with SSI. Only the following items, which Social Security calls "countable" housing expenses, will reduce the SSI benefit:

- Mortgage (principal and interest)
- Rent
- Real estate taxes
- Gas

---

6. This rule, the Presumed Maximum Value Rule, is discussed in detail in the Public Benefits (SSI) section (Chapter 2). However, in Illinois, Indiana, and Wisconsin, there are different rules. In those states, if an SSI recipient pays more than one-third of his monthly income for rent, then additional payments by a third party to the landlord will not reduce SSI. 20 C.F.R.§ 416.1130(b). And, in New York, Connecticut, and Vermont, housing payments made by a third party on behalf of an SSI recipient will not reduce SSI if such payments do not increase the recipient's actual financial ability to purchase housing. "Ruppert v. Bowen" 871 F2d 1172, 1174 (1989).

- Electricity
- Water
- Sewer
- Homeowner's insurance required by a lender
- Condominium charges that include the above items.

416.C.F.R. § 1130(b); POMS SI 00835.465D.

Although Social Security has not expressly identified what housing related expenses are "non-countable" and will *not* cause a problem with SSI, advocates generally agree that the trustee may safely pay for the following items:

- Telephone
- Cable television
- DVD/Video players
- Computer
- Premiums for personal property insurance
- Paper products
- Laundry and cleaning supplies
- Staff salaries
- Repairs to the recipient's home
- Capital improvements to the recipient's home.

If the trustee pays for any *countable* housing items, then SSI will be reduced by the lesser of the item's actual value or one-third of the federal benefit amount, plus $20 (currently $213 in 2005). (This rule, the Presumed Maximum Value Rule, is explained in the SSI section of Public Benefits (Chapter 2).

> For example, John, an SSI recipient, lives in his own apartment. In one month, John's family pays his $250 heating oil bill. That month, John's SSI will be reduced by $213.

> But, the next month, John's family instead pays his $40 electric bill. That month, John's SSI payment will be reduced by only $40.

An important point to keep in mind is that even if the SSI recipient receives more than one countable shelter item in a month, SSI is never reduced by more than $213 per month. This can be important for homeowners if the trustee must pay expenses for mortgage, real estate taxes, homeowner's insurance and utilities every month.

Another important point is that if the trustee pays for a countable shelter item, then it only affects the SSI benefit for one month, which is the month the benefit is received. The SSI benefit for the next month will not be affected.

How can the Trustee assist a beneficiary who rents his own apartment?

If the SSI recipient rents an apartment, then the trustee should not pay for any countable housing expenses such as rent, utilities such as electricity, gas, or oil heat, or for garbage removal. Instead, the trustee may pay for non-countable housing expenses such as telephone, cable television, premiums for personal property (tenant) insurance, and non-food staples such as paper products, and laundry and cleaning supplies. Also, any salaries for residential support staff can be paid by the trustee out of trust funds without affecting the SSI benefit.

> For example, John, an SSI recipient, lives with supervision in his own apartment. If the Trustee pays monthly rent of $450 to the landlord, then John's monthly payment will be reduced by $213. Instead, if John uses his SSI funds to pay his rent and the trustee pays for the staff costs, then SSI will not be reduced, because John has not received outside help with any "countable" shelter costs.

Note that if paying rent to the landlord is a bad idea, giving John money to pay his landlord is a worse idea. As explained throughout this manual, if the trustee gives cash directly to the recipient, then it will be counted as unearned income, in which case SSI will be reduced on a dollar-for-dollar basis.

How can the trustee assist the beneficiary who owns his own home?

If the recipient owns his own home, then the trustee should avoid paying for the mortgage, real estate taxes, homeowner's insurance, utilities, water, sewer, and garbage removal. Of course, this may not be possible if the beneficiary has only limited income and must rely on the trust to pay for his housing costs. In that case, it is almost always preferable for the beneficiary to have his SSI reduced than to lose his home.

Fortunately, there are many housing-related expenses that the trustee can safely pay without affecting the SSI benefit. As with the tenant who rents, the trustee may pay for landscaping and snow removal, telephone, cable television, and non-food items such as paper products and laundry and cleaning supplies. Salaries of residential support staff are permitted expenditures. Also, the trustee can pay for a new roof, construct an addition, make a bathroom accessible, and so forth, without causing SSI to be reduced.

Can monthly housing costs be paid annually to maximize SSI?

No. A creative, but misinformed, trustee might assume that she can easily circumvent the pertinent rules by paying large housing costs on an annual basis. For example, although real estate taxes are usually billed quarterly at $900, for an annual cost of $3,600, the trustee might pay these taxes annually. That way, she thinks, SSI might be reduced only one time per year.

That approach has been foreclosed, however, because Social Security converts any housing bills to monthly amounts, even if these bills are actually paid less frequently. 20 C.F.R. §416.1133(c); POMS SI 00835.474. For example, if an SSI recipient has annual real estate taxes of $3,600, then those taxes are divided by the number of months in the billing period, resulting in monthly taxes of $300. In this example, the SSI recipient has monthly in-kind income of $300.

Who should own the house?

An SSI recipient can own a home. The home is a non-countable asset, regardless of its value, as long as the recipient lives in the home. 20 C.F.R. § 416.1210; POMS SI 01130.100.

A better alternative, however, might be for the SSI recipient's Special Needs Trust to own the home, since home ownership by the Special Needs Trust can offer some potential advantages that ownership by the individual may not provide. For example, the trustee can offer independent management and oversight for the beneficiary who may lack capacity to manage his own property. Also, continuity of ownership can be assured because beneficial ownership can pass, on the beneficiary's death, to named remainder beneficiaries, such as other family members. Another possible advantage, as explained in the Housing Subsidies section below, is that the trustee may be eligible to participate in housing subsidy programs that would not be available if the beneficiary or a close family member owned the house in his own name.

In Massachusetts, if a Special Needs Trust owns real estate, then a trust certificate, which identifies the trustee, is placed on the public record. The Special Needs Trust does not need to be recorded, and thus the identity of the beneficiary and his disability remain private.

Sometimes the Special Needs Trust and an individual, often a family member, own the property together. This situation might occur when both contribute to the cost to purchase, renovate, or maintain the property. In this case, the deed must be carefully drafted to reflect the appropriate ownership interests.

The ownership of real estate gives rise to many complicated legal, public benefit, and estate planning considerations. If the purchase of real estate is contemplated, then an attorney experienced in these matters should be involved in all aspects of the process.

Housing Subsidies

Given the current high cost of housing, many people with disabilities must rely on public housing programs to keep a roof over their heads. Some people with disabilities live in low-cost rental apartments in public housing projects. Others live in private rental housing for which the local public housing authority (PHA) pays a portion of their rent. Both the federal and state governments provide housing assistance, which, not surprisingly, is available only to certain "needy" individuals. This section examines housing subsidies, including the Section 8 program, and discusses how the Special Needs Trust can affect one's eligibility for that program.

In most programs, there are different rules for basic eligibility and for setting the amount of rent. Both sets of rules are discussed below.

How can one qualify for a housing subsidy?

To qualify for federal subsidized housing, one's income cannot exceed 80 percent of the median income in the area. 24 C.F.R. § 5.603. For Massachusetts subsidies, one must have "low income" as defined by regulations enacted by HUD (the Department of Housing and Urban Development). 760 C.M.R. § 5.06. The low- and median-income figures, which are adjusted by HUD on April 1 of each year, can be obtained from the HUD website (located in the Appendix) or from any local housing authority office.

As compared to SSI, HUD's definition of "low income" is relatively generous. HUD defines "low income" as earning less than 30% of the median income for your area. Because this definition is based on the local median income, the actual figures for "low income" qualification vary from place to place. For example, while the HUD definition of "low income" may be relatively high for those residing in Boston ($46,300 in 2005), it is lower in a city such as Pittsfield, with a "low income" level of $34,550 in 2005.

Are there any asset limits?

No. There are no asset limits for participation in most federal and Massachusetts housing subsidy programs. Thus, the amount of assets an applicant owns will not affect his eligibility for a housing subsidy. However, as discussed below, in some cases, income generated by one's assets is considered countable income for program purposes, which affects eligibility.

Does income affect eligibility?

Yes. Eligibility for subsidized housing is based on the family's annual income, as defined by HUD. Annual income includes items such as earnings from employment and self-employment; public benefits such as SSI, SSDI, and certain welfare payments; pensions and retirements; unemployment compensation; alimony and child support; and regular gifts and contributions from persons not residing with the family.

Also, annual income may include earnings generated by family assets. The general rule is that if "family assets," as defined by HUD, are less than $5,000, then any income produced by those assets (such as interest and dividends) is disregarded in determining eligibility. However, if total family assets exceed $5,000, then income earned by those assets will be counted. HUD uses the greater of actual earnings or the "passbook rate" as set by HUD. 24 C.F.R. § 609(b)(3). In 2005, the passbook rate is about one percent.

If an applicant or participant transfers an asset for less than its fair market value, then, for two years after the transfer, HUD will treat the asset as if it were still owned by the participant and will assume that the asset earns interest at the passbook rate. 24 C.F.R. 5.603(b)(3).

> For example, John, a subsidized tenant, inherits $100,000 and places that amount into a Special Needs Trust. For the next two years, HUD will assume that John has interest income on $100,000 at the passbook rate. (HUD's treatment of earnings from a Special Needs Trust is discussed below.)

Some examples of *non-countable* income are lump sum additions to family assets, such as inheritances and insurance settlements for losses; any amounts received specifically for, or as reimbursement of, medical expenses for the family; amounts received by an SSI recipient that are disregarded as income by SSI because they are set aside for a PASS (discussed in the "Work" section (Chapter 5)); and income received from certain work training programs funded by HUD. Also, the income of a live-in aide, such as a Personal Care Attendant who provides necessary support services for a tenant with disabilities, is not considered income for program purposes. 24 C.R.F. §§ 5.609(c); 982.316.

Does a Special Needs Trust affect eligibility?

No. Funds held in a Special Needs Trust are specifically excluded from the definition of family assets and are disregarded for eligibility purposes. Also, any *income* earned by the trust, such as interest and dividends, is disregarded, so long as that income is held in the trust and not distributed. However, if any trust income is distributed directly to the beneficiary, then it is considered countable income for program purposes. Thus, the trustee should not distribute trust income directly to the beneficiary. 24 C.F.R. § 5.603(b)(2).

What can the trustee safely pay for?

Unfortunately, the rules in this area are not very clear. Thus, the trustee must proceed cautiously, since the interpretation by the local public housing authorities may vary.

It is generally agreed, however, that distributions for the beneficiary's uninsured medical expenses are not counted as income. This is true even if the distribution is made directly to the beneficiary, instead of to a third party, such as the medical provider.

Also, occasional distributions for items such as a vacation or purchase of an automobile would probably not be considered income, nor would occasional miscellaneous purchases such as a health club membership or holiday gifts. And an emergency expenditure, such as payment of a large overdue electric bill or oil bill, would probably not cause a problem.

What should the trustee *not* pay for?

The trustee should avoid making regular distributions from the trust directly to the beneficiary. For example, the trustee should not give the beneficiary a monthly cash distribution, as this would probably be considered income for program purposes. Also, the trustee should avoid making regular payments from the trust for the tenant/beneficiary's benefit. For example, if the trustee pays the beneficiary's monthly rent or utility charges, then this would probably be considered income. As a practical matter, however, it may not be possible for the trustee to avoid paying these charges if the beneficiary must rely on the trust fund for all or part of his housing expenses.

The effect of trust distributions on a Section 8 recipient's eligibility is a complicated area where even knowledgeable advocates sometimes disagree. The safest course of action for the trustee is to discuss this situation with an attorney experienced in this area or with the local PHA to learn how its rules are applied.

How is the tenant's rent determined?

For most federal programs, tenants pay 30 percent of adjusted family income, as defined by HUD. In Massachusetts, most tenants in state programs pay 25 percent to 30 percent of adjusted family income, depending on whether utilities are included in the rent. For purposes of setting the rent, trust distributions are included in the definition of income just as they were taken into account for program eligibility.

As with the program eligibility rules, *income* earned by funds held in a Special Needs Trust is excluded, unless it is distributed directly to the beneficiary, in which case it is counted as income. Also, in some circumstances, other types of distributions from the trust may be counted. Thus, if there are significant distributions in any year, that may increase the beneficiary's share of the rent. 24 C.F.R. § 5.603; 760 C.M.R. § 5.06.

The Section 8 Program

What is the Section 8 program?

In the Northeast United States, an important source of decent, safe, and affordable housing for low-income people with disabilities is the so-called Section 8 Program.[7] That program, which is funded with federal money and administered by HUD, is managed at the state and local levels primarily by public housing authorities (PHA's). These PHA's provide rental vouchers to persons who meet the eligibility rules established by HUD.[8]

What is a Section 8 voucher?

A Section 8 arrangement involves a three-party agreement among the tenant, the PHA, and a participating landlord who owns private rental housing. The tenant pays a portion of his income (30 percent in most cases), and the PHA pays the remaining rent (the voucher amount) directly to the landlord.

---

7. The formal name is the Housing Choice Voucher Program (HCVP).

8. There are currently four types of housing assistance provided by the Section 8 program: tenant-based rental assistance, project-based rental assistance, home-ownership assistance, and down payment assistance. This section discusses only the tenant-based rental assistance portion of the program. For an excellent guide to all four parts of the Section 8 program, see *Section 8 Made Simple*, published by the Technical Assistance Collaborative, Inc., listed in "Where to Go for Help section (Chapter 12).

Section 8 vouchers can be either "mobile" or "project-based." Mobile vouchers belong to the tenant, so that the tenant can take the voucher to a new apartment if he moves. Project-based vouchers are attached to apartments and do not move with the tenant.

How much rent can the landlord charge?

The maximum rent that the landlord can charge for any particular unit is set by the local PHA according to certain "payment standards," using HUD guidelines. These payment standards, which are reflective of modestly priced rental units in the local area, are based on the number of bedrooms in the unit. For example, there is a payment standard for a studio apartment, one-bedroom unit, two-bedroom unit, and so forth. The rent charged by the landlord cannot exceed the payment standard for the unit's size.

Not surprisingly, given the diverse housing market conditions within most states, there can often be a relatively wide range of payment standards. In Massachusetts, for example, in the first part of 2005, the payment standard for a one-bedroom apartment was $1077 in Boston, $701 in Worcester, and $517 in Pittsfield. The current regional payment standards for all 50 states, which are adjusted on October 1 each year, can be obtained from the HUD website (see Appendix) or from any PHA office.

Once these annual payment standards have been established, they are not set in stone. The PHA has some flexibility to approve a higher payment standard, on a case by case basis, as a reasonable accommodation for a person with a disability. 24 C.F.R. § 982.505(d). For example, the PHA could approve a fully accessible apartment that costs more than a non-accessible unit for a person with a disability who needs that type of accommodation.

How much rent does the tenant pay?

In general, the tenant pays 30 percent of his income as rent, and the housing authority pays the balance of the rent directly to the landlord.

> For example, John, who has SSDI and earnings of $1,400 per month, is approved for a one-bedroom apartment which rents for $900 per month. The $900 rental amount is within the payment standard set by

the PHA. Thus, John would pay $420 per month ($1,400 x 30%) to the landlord, and the housing authority would pay $480.

However, the tenant can choose an apartment that costs more than the payment standard for a comparable apartment in the area. In that case, the PHA will still pay only the difference between 30 percent of the tenant's income and the payment standard. In addition to paying 30 percent of his income for rent, the tenant must also pay the difference between the payment standard and the actual rent.

> For example, John has SSDI and earnings of $1,400 per month. The payment standard for an apartment in John's area is $900 per month, but he chooses to rent an apartment that costs $1,000 per month. The housing authority pays $480, and John must pay $520 ($420 + $100).

The tenant's right to choose a more expensive apartment is not unlimited, however. According to section 8 program rules, in most cases a tenant cannot pay more than 40 percent of his income toward rent. Thus, in the above example, the PHA would not approve an apartment that cost $1,200 per month, because then John's share of the rent would amount to $720, which is 51 percent of his income.

There is an exception to the 40 percent rule for existing Section 8 tenants where the landlord increases the rent (with the permission of the PHA). In that case, the PHA might approve the higher tenant payment as long as the rent charged by the landlord is reasonable.

Can a family member be the section 8 landlord?

In most cases, no. That has not always been the case, however. Before a recent (April 1999) change in the law, a person could rent his or her own property to a family member with a disability, and the local housing authority would pay a portion of the family member's rent.

Under the old law, a typical arrangement involved a parent renting an apartment in his or her own house (including a so-called in-law apartment) to a son or daughter with a disability. However, under the current law, this arrangement is prohibited, because the owner may not be the parent, child, grandparent, grandchild, sister, or brother of any member of the family.

There is an exception if this arrangement is needed as a "reasonable accommodation" for the disabled family member. 24 C.F.R. § 982.306(d). Although the regulations do not give any examples of a "reasonable accommodation," some advocates suggest that a duplex or two-family property occupied by both the parent and a disabled family member who needs 24-hour supervision might qualify.

There is another exception for family ownership arrangements that were in existence before the April 1999 change in the law. Those arrangements have been "grandfathered" and may continue to exist under the new law.

Can the Special Needs Trust be the section 8 landlord?

Yes, provided that the trust owns the beneficiary's residence. The trustee can even be the parent or other close family member of the disabled tenant/beneficiary, because the Special Needs Trust, which is a separate legal entity, is not subject to the rules that prohibit most family landlord-tenant rental arrangements. (However, there may be sound public benefits and "family dynamics" reasons why there should be an independent trustee who is not related to the beneficiary.)

Although a section 8 arrangement can be quite complicated to administer, if successful, it can provide a significant economic benefit to the beneficiary.

Briefly, it works this way. The beneficiary, as the tenant, obtains a housing subsidy from her local PHA. The trustee, as landlord, agrees to participate in the housing subsidy program and enters into a written lease agreement with the beneficiary and the PHA. The beneficiary pays 30 percent of his income as rent, and the PHA pays the remaining rent to the trustee.

This arrangement helps the beneficiary by reducing his monthly rent. Also, the trust benefits from an increased income stream.

CHAPTER 4

RECREATION

Most people with disabilities like to go out and have fun. Money in a special needs trust can help them do that. It can pay for items like a restaurant meal, vacation, or night out on the town. But some advocates claim that Social Security does not like people with disabilities to have too much fun. They warn that every recreational expense may be scrutinized by an overzealous caseworker. As a result, some trustees are reluctant to spend *any* money on recreation for fear of getting into trouble with Social Security. This chapter explains how the trustee can help the beneficiary have fun, while avoiding missteps that could risk the SSI benefit.

What rules govern recreation costs?

To appreciate how recreation costs can cause a problem with SSI, it helps to understand both how that program counts income, and what happens if a recipient has too much income. As we explain throughout this manual SSI is a "need based" program that is available only to individuals who have few resources and very low income. Once a person is approved for SSI and begins to receive cash benefits, the Social Security case workers can from time to time thoroughly review item the person receives. Usually these reviews take place annually. The workers are looking for any cash, food, and shelter items that the person may have received from third parties. Food and shelter, which Social Security calls "in-kind income," are "not cash but (are) actually food or shelter or something (you) can use to get one of these. 20 C.F.R. sec. 416.1102.

If Social Security learns that a recipient has received any cash, food, or shelter (or its equivalent), the SSI benefit may be reduced.[9] The amount of the reduction

---

9. However, in-kind income is not a problem for every SSI recipient. Some SSI recipients live in the household of another person who provides both food and shelter (such as a child who lives with his or her parents). These recipient already get a reduced benefit. Therefore, even if they receive additional food or shelter, their benefit will not be reduced further. This is explained in the Public Benefits section (SSI) of Chapter 2.

depends on the kind and amount of income. If the recipient receives more than $20 per month in cash, he will lose one dollar of SSI for every dollar of cash received. If he receives a food or shelter item, his SSI payment will be reduced by the lesser of the item's value or $213 (in 2005). (These rules are discussed in detail in Chapter 2.)

While these rules may sound harsh, their application is not necessarily overly severe. This is because SSI counts income on a month-to-month basis. If there is excess income in any one month, SSI is reduced *only for that one month*. The next month's benefit is not affected.

Also, if there is any in-kind income, the monthly benefit is never reduced by more than $213, no matter how great the expenditure. And as a practical matter, most recreational items will not cost more than $213 in any one month.

Last, trustees should note that Social Security's definition of income is not necessarily limited to cash, food, and shelter items. In-kind income can also include "something (one) can use to get food or shelter." There is an unsettling example in the POMS (the Social Security workers' manual) that states that if an SSI recipient receives a certain kind of airplane ticket that could potentially be redeemed for cash, he has received in-kind income. POMS SI 01120.150. This example if quite disturbing, because, if taken to its logical extreme, almost any kind of property could be sold and converted to cash. Fortunately, this airplane-tickets-for-cash example does not appear anywhere else in the POMS. Nevertheless, trustees must still be careful about their recreational expenditures.

The following are some strategies that trustees have successfully used.

What recreational expenses may be trustee pay?

Paid Companions: To enjoy a community experience, some individuals with disabilities may require one-to-one assistance from specially trained staff. These paid companions are usually compensated on an hourly basis. The use of trust funds for paid companions does not cause a problem with SSI.

Gifts: Some beneficiaries like to give inexpensive gifts to friends or family members on birthdays, holidays, or other special occasions. This should not cause a problem with SSI because a third party, not the beneficiary, receives the purchased item.

Club Memberships: Some people with disabilities belong to local health clubs and Family YMCAs. The trustee may use trust funds to pay for these memberships.

Movie and Concert Tickets: Some popular recreational activities are going to movies, concerts, and sports events. The trustee can use trust funds to purchase tickets. However, if possible, she should avoid giving the money directly to the recipient. Instead, she could purchase tickets and reimburse herself from the trust funds. Alternatively, she could give the money to buy tickets to the person's staff.

Restaurant Meals: Most people with disabilities like to eat out. However, *paying* for the meals can be troublesome for the trustee, because an SSI recipient is not supposed to get any food items from a third party source, including his special needs trust. However, the following strategies might work.

For an occasional meal, the trustee can simply give the beneficiary $20. The program rules allow a person to receive $20 in any one month without penalty. In addition to $20 per month, a person may also receive another $20 in any calendar quarter (every three months). 416 C.M.R. sec. 1124(c)(6);SI 00810.410.

If more money is needed, perhaps the meal could be "repackaged." One of the authors regularly pays for her client's restaurant dinners from trust funds. She creatively characterizes these meals as "therapeutic milieu experiences." Social Security has never challenged this arrangement.

Vacations and Travel: Some enterprising travel agents offer package vacations specially adapted for people with disabilities. These include weekends in the country, overnight trips to vacation resorts, and even luxury cruises. Usually there is a single charge that covers transportation, lodging, meals, and other amenities.

Here the obvious problem is that a vacation package includes both food and shelter, which Social Security says is prohibited. We are aware of a situation where a parent, just back from a Florida family vacation, was grilled by an overly inquisitive case worker about how much was spent on every meal, airplane snack, and hotel room for the man's disabled adult daughter. While the daughter's SSI benefit was not ultimately affected, the parent was understandably rattled.

Fortunately, Social Security no longer pursues benefit reduction if a person goes on vacation. The current rules allow a recipient to receive both food and shelter during a temporary absence from home, such as a vacation. A temporary absence is one of at least 24 hours duration. 20 C.F.R. sec. 416.1149; POMS SI 00835.040.

CHAPTER 5

WORK

Although the general requirement to receive SSI or SSDI is that one must be unable to engage in substantial gainful employment, many recipients work to help support themselves. To encourage people with disabilities to work, Social Security has developed several important work incentive programs that allow recipients to work but still keep some or all of their public benefits. However, there are important differences in the way that Social Security treats earned income, depending on whether one participates in the SSI or SSDI program. This section examines how both the SSI and SSDI programs treat earned income and how work incentives can be used to increase the aggregate income for recipients in both programs.

We also discuss two work incentive programs, namely Impairment-Related Work Incentives and the PASS. Although other work incentive programs may be helpful to the beneficiary, those two programs were selected because they are the only such programs that may be affected by the Special Needs Trust funds.[10] Lastly, we explain why the beneficiary should pay for work-related expenses with his personal funds and why the trustee should *not* pay for work-related expenses with trust assets.

What are Work Incentives?

To encourage people to work, Social Security has developed certain "work incentive" programs. These work incentives allow Social Security to disregard some or all of the recipient's earnings when it calculates his benefit. Work

---

10. For a thorough discussion of all the work incentive programs, including work subsidies, excluded student earnings, and the new "Ticket to Work," see An Advocate's Guide to Surviving the SSI System, by Linda L. Landry, et al, or "The Red Book on Employment," Social Security Publication No. 64-030. Both publications are listed in the "Where to Go for Help." Section (Chapter 12).

incentives are important because they allow some recipients who work to keep all of their earnings *and* some or all of their government benefit.

Some work incentive programs apply only to SSI recipients, some apply only to those who get SSDI, and some apply to both. For example, the most common work incentive under the SSI program allows Social Security to disregard the first $65 of a recipient's earned income, plus one-half of the remaining earned income. Using this "earned income exclusion," SSI recipients who work can keep a portion of their benefit and, most importantly, continue to qualify for Medicaid. Although the earned income exclusion applies only to SSI and not to SSDI, another important work incentive program, "impairment-related work expenses," is available to recipients in both programs.

To appreciate how work incentives can help both SSI and SSDI recipients, it is necessary to understand how those two programs treat earned income. The rules are different for each program, and the effect of a work incentive on the recipient's benefit may be different, depending on whether one gets SSI or SSDI. Those differences are summarized below.

How does Earned Income affect the SSI and SSDI Benefit?

The following are the rules SSI and SSDI uses if the recipient has earned income:

The SSI Calculation: If an SSI recipient earns more than $20 per month, then his SSI benefit will be reduced. To calculate the reduction, Social Security subtracts from the individual's total monthly earned income the general exclusion of $20 (if not used on unearned income), the first $65 of earned income, any impairment related work expenses (discussed in the next section), and one-half of remaining earned income. If the remaining earned income is *less* than the maximum SSI benefit amount for his SSI payment level, then that income is subtracted from the maximum benefit amount, and the recipient keeps the reduced SSI payment. But, if the remaining earned income *exceeds* the maximum SSI benefit amount, then the individual has too much income and cannot get SSI.

For example, John lives with his girlfriend and earns $200 per month from employment. The maximum SSI benefit amount for John's payment level is $609.40. John's SSI benefit is calculated as follows:

$200.00   earned income
-$20.00   SSI General Exclusion
$180.00
-$65.00   SSI Earned Income Exclusion
$115.00
-$57.50   one-half of remaining earned income
$57.50   total countable earned income

Then,

$609.40   maximum SSI benefit amount (in 2005)
-$57.50   total countable earned income
$551.90   reduced SSI benefit

John now has $751.90 available for his support (wages of $200 plus reduced SSI benefit of $551.90).

The SSDI Calculation: As with SSI, the SSDI calculation begins with the individual's total monthly earned income from all sources. But, unlike SSI, the SSDI program has neither a $20 general exclusion nor an earned income exclusion. Any work incentives, such as the impairment related work incentives (discussed later in this section) are subtracted from earned income to arrive at one's "total countable earned income." If that figure is below the SGA (Substantial Gainful Activity)[11] level for the individual's category, then the recipient keeps his *full* SSDI benefit. (Note that SSDI benefits, unlike SSI payments, are never partially reduced.) However, if earned income *exceeds* the SGA level, then SSDI is *eliminated* and the recipient loses his *entire* benefit.

For example, John has SSDI of $900 per month and earnings of $750 per month. Since SSDI has no $20 general exclusion and no earned income exclusion, and in our example John has no impairment related work expenses, John's total countable earned income is therefore $750 per month. Since $750 is less than the SGA level of $830, John is eligible for SSDI. He can keep *both* all of his earnings *and* his full SSDI benefit of $900 per month. But, if John earned $830 or more per

---

11. As explained in the public benefits section of this manual, SGA is an earnings level that Social Security uses to determine if one is unable to work and therefore "disabled." In 2005, that earnings level is $830 for a non-blind person and $1,380 for a blind person.

month, then he would lose SSDI, since his earnings exceed the SGA level for his category.

What are Impairment-Related Work Expenses, and how can they assist the SSI and SSDI recipient?

Impairment-related work expenses (called by the strange sounding acronym IRWE) are defined by program rules as certain items or services that an SSI or SSDI recipient must have, because of his disability, in order to work. 20 C.F.R. §§ 404.1576, 416.976.

A recipient can use his impairment-related work expenses to reduce his countable income and retain some or all of his government benefits.

For example, John, an SSI recipient, earns $500 per month in supported employment and has IRWE of $100 per month. The maximum SSI benefit amount for John's category is $609.40.

$500.00	earned income	
-$20.00	SSI General Exclusion	
$480.00		
-$65.00	SSI Earned Income Exclusion	
$415.00		
-$100.00	IRWE	
$315.00		
-$157.50	one-half of remaining earned income	
$157.50	total countable earned income	

Thus, John would receive:

$609.40	maximum SSI benefit amount (in 2005)
-$157.50	total countable earned income
$451.90	reduced SSI benefit

Although John's SSI benefit is slightly *decreased*, his total income has *increased*. When we add reduced SSI of $451.90 to his earned income of $500 and subtract impairment-related work expenses of $100, John now has $851.90 available for his self-support.

If, in the above example, John receives SSDI of $582.40, then his total income will be $982.40 (SSDI of $582.40, plus earnings of $500, less IRWE of $100). Since John's total countable earnings of $400 are less than the SGA level of $830, John can keep his entire SSDI benefit.

What are some examples of IRWE?

To qualify as an IRWE, the pertinent rules state that the person with disabilities must need the item or service in order to work because of his physical or mental impairment, and the item or service must be directly related to his work. In some cases, however, the person might also require the item or service for his every-day living needs. In that situation, only the work related portion of the item of service is deductible. Also, the rules require that the recipient must *personally* pay for the cost of the item or service. No deduction will be allowed if payment has been made by an outside source, including a Special Needs Trust, or if it is reimbursed by insurance. The following are some examples of deductible IRWE's:

Attendant Care Services. Attendants (called Personal Care Attendants, or PCA's in Massachusetts), perform a variety of tasks required to help the recipient meet his essential personal needs at home or work, such as bathing, toileting, dressing, cooking, eating, communicating, traveling to and from work, and so forth. Only the portion of the attendant's services that actually enable the recipient to work is deductible as IRWE. The POMS (Procedures Operation Manual System) offers some examples: attendant services needed at work; or to help the recipient get from home to work, or from work to home; or to assist the recipient in preparation for work, or upon his return home from work (but, only for one to two hours in the morning or evening). Attendant care services performed on non-work days, or services performed at any time that involve shopping or general homemaking (e.g. cleaning or laundry) are *not* deductible.

Medical Devices. Medical devices are defined as durable medical equipment that can stand repeated uses and serve a medical purpose. Medical devices such as wheelchairs, canes, pacemakers, inhalators, and prosthetic devices may be permitted deductions if the recipient must have them in order to work.

Adapted Work-Related Equipment. Expenses for equipment that the worker with disabilities needs to perform his job and are not provided by his employer are deductible. Some examples are telecommunications devices for the deaf, reading aids for the blind, and tools specially adapted to accommodate the worker's impairment.

Residential Modifications. Certain alterations to the *exterior* of the worker's home may be deductible expenses. To qualify, such alterations must be needed to help the worker access transportation to and from work. Some examples are wheelchair ramps, special stair rails, or pathways for someone who uses crutches. But, modifications to the *interior* of the home that assist the individual to function at home, such as large doorframes, lower kitchen counters and appliances, special bathroom facilities, and so forth, are *not* deductible.

Routine Drugs and Medical Services. The costs of routine drugs and routine medical services are deductible if they are necessary to control the worker's disabling condition, thereby enabling him to work. Some examples of deductible medical expenses are anticonvulsant drugs and related diagnostic blood monitoring tests for workers with epilepsy or seizure disorders; radiation treatment or chemotherapy for cancer patients; corrective surgery and physical therapy for spinal disorders; anti-depressant medications for workers with mental illness; and optical treatment for a worker with a disabling visual impairment. But, routine medical costs for services not directly related to the worker's physical impairment, such as routine physical exams, dental care, and eyeglasses, are not deductible expenses.

Guide Dog. A blind person's expenses for his guide dog, including the cost of purchasing the dog, dog food, a license, and veterinary care are deductible.

Transportation. If the worker can use regular public transportation, then those transportation expenses are *not* deductible. But, if the worker cannot use public transportation because of his impairment, for example he uses a wheelchair and no accessible public transportation is available, or he has cognitive disabilities and cannot navigate public transportation, then the costs of his special transportation may be deductible. In that case, alternative transportation such as driver assistance and taxicabs would be deductible. If a worker requires a specially adapted or modified vehicle in order to work, then the cost of the modification (but not the vehicle itself) is deductible, as are operating costs at a mileage rate specified by Social Security. Lastly, if a worker drives an unadapted vehicle to work, no deduction may be taken, even if there is no public transportation available where he lives. Ref. 20 C.F.R. §§ 404.976; 416.1576.

How can the trustee assist an SSI recipient who has impairment related work expenses?

To be deductible, an IRWE must be paid for by the recipient. No deduction is permitted if the item or service is paid for by a third party. Accordingly, in order to maximize the SSI or SSDI recipient's benefit, the trustee should *not* pay for *any* items or services that could qualify as impairment related work expenses. The recipient will lose the IRWE deduction and not receive the maximum benefit. Instead, the recipient should pay for these items and services from his own income.

How can the PASS Program assist an SSI recipient?

A Plan for Achieving Self-Support (PASS) is a work incentive program that allows an SSI recipient to keep income and/or resources while working toward a vocational goal. Persons who use a PASS can keep some or all of their SSI benefit as they work toward self-support, even though they would otherwise earn too much or have too many resources to get public benefits. To qualify, a PASS must:

- Be designated specifically for the person's needs, goals, abilities, and circumstances;

- Be in writing and signed by the person for whom it is written;

- Have a designated and feasible work goal;

- Have a time table for achieving the work goal (a PASS can be designated for an initial period of up to 18 months, with additional extensions for up to 48 months total);

- Show what other income and resources the person has and how those will be used to achieve the work goal; and

- Show how money set aside as resources will be kept identified from any other resources the person may have.

42 U.S.C.§ 1382a(b)(4); 20 C.F.R. § 416.1180.

For example, Megan, a 32 year old woman with mental illness who receives SSI of $693.39 per month, wants to begin training to work as a veterinarian's assistant and, eventually, to become self-supporting. To reach her goal, she will need both the services of a job coach and public transportation to and from work, at a total cost of $390 per month.

Megan expects to reach her goal in 18 months. While training, she will earn $800 per month. Megan's PASS calculations are as follows:

$800.00	salary
-$20.00	SSI General Exclusion
$780.00	
-$65.00	SSI Earned Income Exclusion
$715.00	
-$357.50	one-half of remaining earned income
$357.00	
-$390.00	job coach and transportation
(-32.50)	total countable earned income

Since Megan has no countable income, she can keep her entire SSI check. Thus, when we add SSI of $693.39 to earned income of $800, and subtract PASS expenses of $390, Megan has $1,103.39 available for her self-support during job training.

Can one have both a PASS and a Special Needs Trust?

There are no specific regulations that address whether a person with disabilities can have both a PASS and a Special Needs Trust. However, in a recent case involving an SSI recipient who has a Special Needs Trust, the Boston Social Security Office denied a proposed PASS, saying that the recipient could not have both a Special Needs Trust and a PASS. The basis was that trust funds were available to pay for all of the proposed items and services in the PASS, including a job coach, uniforms, and special work-related materials. Also, Social Security pointed out that the use of trust funds for those types of expenses would not cause a reduction in SSI benefits.

Thus, before undertaking the effort to write a PASS, a beneficiary should first discuss this situation with his local society security office. He should ask whether his plan is likely to be rejected solely because he has a Special Needs Trust.

CHAPTER 6

MEDICAL EXPENSES

Many people with disabilities have significant medical needs. Fortunately, in most states, people with disabilities can easily obtain Medicaid insurance, which generally pays for one hundred percent of "covered" services. But due to the current nationwide budget crisis, the number of "covered" services is shrinking at an alarming rate.[12] Thus, the trustee may sometimes be asked to disburse funds from the Special Needs Trust to pay for the beneficiary's medical services that are not covered by insurance. This section discusses what expenses the trustee should pay from trust funds, and which ones she should not pay.

How can the Special Needs Trust help with medical expenses?

In most cases, paying the beneficiary's medical expenses from trust funds does not create a problem with SSI. Program rules allow an SSI recipient to receive outside help with medical costs without affecting his SSI benefit.

This is fortunate, because even if the beneficiary has Medicaid, that program does not always cover every medical item or service that the beneficiary may need. In some cases, psychological services, certain types of testing, and some special therapies are not covered expenses. For example, in Massachusetts, the state has limited payment for Personal Care Attendants (PCA's), individuals who provide assistance with daily needs such as bathing, cooking, transfers, and so forth. If the PCA provides "skilled care," then her services are covered, but if the PCA provides only routine or "unskilled care," then it can be harder to obtain Medicaid reimbursement.

---

12. For example, in 2002, Massachusetts eliminated eyeglasses, prosthetic devices, and most routine dental care for many Medicaid recipients.

For some Medicaid recipients, the problem is finding a medical provider that accepts Medicaid. In Massachusetts, for example, few dentists participate in the Medicaid program because of the low rates of reimbursement. Thus, some Medicaid recipients are accustomed to paying for dental care out of their personal funds. Some Medicaid recipients, for personal reasons such as a longstanding relationship with a doctor who does not accept Medicaid, may voluntarily pay for that doctor out of their personal funds, even though a Medicaid-insured physician is available. In these cases, the use of trust funds to pay for medical items and services is appropriate.

If the beneficiary does not have Medicaid, then trust funds can be used to purchase medical insurance and pay for co-payments, deductibles and other out of pocket medical costs. These payments will not reduce the SSI benefit.

However, the trustee must be careful *how* she pays for medical costs. The trustee should pay the provider directly and *not* give the beneficiary funds to pay any medical bills. If the trustee gives money directly to the beneficiary, then that would be considered *unearned income*. Unearned income of more than $20 per month will reduce and possibly eliminate the SSI benefit.

What medical costs should the trustee *not* pay?

As explained in the "Work" section (Chapter 5) of this manual, some SSI and SSDI recipients who work may need certain medical related items or services in order to work. (These items or services are called Impairment-Related Work Expenses, or IRWE's.) For example, the recipient might need an attendant to help him with bathing and dressing before work, or he might need a wheelchair. If those items or services are not covered by any medical insurance and the recipient must pay for them personally, then in some cases Social Security will deduct all or a portion of the cost of those items from his earnings when it calculates his benefit. This is important, because such deductions permit SSI and SSDI recipients to keep more of their earnings, while retaining their government benefit. But to qualify for the deduction, such medical expenses must be paid by the recipient personally and not by an outside source, including a Special Needs Trust. (A sample calculation using IRWE's is illustrated in the "Work" section (Chapter 5) of this manual.)

Accordingly, if the beneficiary has any deductible work-related medical expenses, then in order to maximize the SSI or SSDI benefit, the trustee should *not* pay for these expenses with trust funds. Instead, if possible, the beneficiary should pay for those expenses from his earnings.

CHAPTER 7

TRANSPORTATION

Most people with disabilities need to get out and about, and many need special transportation to do so. In this section, we discuss some common transportation issues that can arise, including payment of transportation costs by a Special Needs Trust and ownership of a specially-adapted vehicle. We also examine a troublesome situation with automobile sales and excise taxes in Massachusetts that prompts some families to place title to expensive adapted vehicles directly in the name of their minor children with disabilities.

Does using trust funds for transportation affect SSI?

No. In general, the use of trust funds for transportation expenses does not cause a problem for the SSI recipient. SSI rules allow a recipient to get financial help with transportation from outside sources without penalty. However, the trustee must be careful about *how* she releases money for transportation costs. The trustee should *not* give money for transportation directly to the beneficiary. As explained in other sections of this manual, any payments of cash made directly to the beneficiary are considered to be unearned income. Unearned income of more than $20 per month will cause the SSI benefit to be reduced or potentially eliminated.

Instead, if possible, the trustee should pay the transportation provider directly. If the beneficiary uses *private transportation,* payment can be arranged directly with the vendor. If the recipient uses *public transportation*, the trustee can purchase tickets or tokens for the recipient. In eastern Massachusetts, tickets for public transportation for people with disabilities (The Ride) can be purchased by mail from the MBTA. If transportation costs are modest, the beneficiary can pay for them himself out of his SSI funds.

How can the Special Needs Trust help a beneficiary who owns a car?

Some individuals with disabilities own their own cars. The SSI rules specifically allow a recipient to own an automobile and there is no longer a limit on the value of the automobile.

The trustee may use trust funds to pay for gas, maintenance, repairs, or insurance without disrupting SSI eligibility. To avoid giving money for gas directly to the beneficiary, the trustee could provide the beneficiary with a gas credit card and pay the charges out of trust funds. Of course, the beneficiary should not use the card to make cash advances, as that would cause a problem with SSI.

If the beneficiary wants to purchase a new or used automobile, then funds to purchase the vehicle should be given directly to the seller and not to the beneficiary directly, so as not to disrupt SSI.

If the recipient's vehicle breaks down and needs to be replaced, then in that limited situation, the trustee may give trust funds for a replacement vehicle directly to the recipient without violating SSI rules. An SSI recipient may personally receive and retain funds earmarked specifically for a "non-countable" resource, such as an automobile. The funds must generally be used within nine months of receipt. 20 C.F. R. § 416.1103(c); POMS SI 01130.630.

But although the rules permit the recipient to retain such funds in this situation, we strongly recommend that the trustee deal directly with the seller and not give funds to the recipient, even for a brief period of time and for a specific identified purpose. Social Security is likely to find out about the excess resources, which could cause an unnecessary headache for the trustee and a potential disruption in benefits for the recipient.

Is it possible to avoid paying sales and excise taxes for an adapted vehicle?

In Massachusetts, the automobile sales tax and excise taxes are a concern for families whose children with disabilities need specially adapted vehicles. The sales tax amounts to 5 percent of the vehicle sales price, and the annual excise tax is assessed at the rate of $25 per $1,000 of value. Since specially adapted vehicles, such as those equipped with a lift mechanism, can cost upwards of $40,000, the excise tax can potentially cost more than $1,000 per year. Similarly, the sales tax can easily exceed $2,000.

Both the sales tax and the excise tax are waived for *owners* of adapted vehicles whose disabling condition meets certain criteria (M.G.L. Ch. 64H(u) and M.G.L. Ch. 60A, Sec.1). Essentially, the law requires that the vehicle's owner must have lost the use of his arms or legs. But what if the vehicle is purchased by the family of a *child* with disabilities? In other words, if the parent of a child with disabilities purchases and registers the vehicle, is there any way for the parent to avoid paying the full sales and excise taxes?

Some families, acting on the advice of salespeople, place title to the adapted vehicle directly in the name of the child with disabilities. This approach avoids the excise and sales taxes, but some attorneys feel it can potentially cause other legal problems for the family.

Fortunately, in March, 2002, the Massachusetts Department of Revenue (DOR), the agency charged with administering the sales tax, reportedly relaxed its requirement that the child with disabilities must be the registered owner (or co-owner) in order to claim the sales tax exemption. According to an internal DOR memorandum that has not been circulated to the public, the DOR now requires only that the parent of a minor child with disabilities for whom the adapted vehicle was purchased be the registered owner.

This is a welcome change as far as the *sales tax* is concerned, but unfortunately, the cities and towns of the Commonwealth that collect *excise taxes* continue to adhere to a strict interpretation of the statute. Specifically, cities and towns do not waive excise taxes unless the minor child with disabilities is the registered owner. Some parents have even been advised by their tax assessor's office that if the child's name is added to the title as a co-owner with the parent, then one-half of the tax will be waived.

What should the family do in this situation? Some attorneys might advise the family that it is all right to make the minor child the owner of the vehicle in order to get the benefit of the tax savings. Other attorneys point out that in Massachusetts children cannot legally transfer title to property, and thus if the child dies or the vehicle must be sold, then expensive court proceedings could be required to address the title problem. What is apparent is that this is a complicated area and the family should discuss their situation with an attorney before proceeding, preferably before the vehicle is purchased.

Are there any circumstances when the trustee should *not* pay for transportation costs?

As explained in the "Work" section (Chapter 5) of this manual, some SSI and SSDI recipients who work may incur "special" transportation expenses getting to and from work, for items such as modifications to an adapted vehicle, a mileage allowance if one's own vehicle is used, driver assistance, or taxicab fare if one cannot use regular public transportation.[13] (Note that regular public transportation does not get any special treatment, only "special" transportation that is needed if the recipient, because of his disability, cannot use regular public transportation.)

Both SSI and SSDI rules state that in some cases a recipient's special transportation costs may be deducted from his gross earnings in calculating his benefit. This is important, because as earnings *increase*, the SSI award is *reduced* and may vanish altogether if earnings are too high. Like SSI, the SSDI benefit may be totally eliminated if earnings exceed program limits. But when special transportation costs are subtracted from earnings, then earnings are lower, and the potential adverse effect on SSI and SSDI is minimized.

Thus, if the SSI or SSDI recipient has work-related special transportation costs, then the trustee should *not* pay for these transportation costs out of trust funds. Doing so will cause the beneficiary to lose the deduction and potentially reduce the benefit amount. Instead, if possible, the recipient should pay for the costs personally out of his SSI or SSDI stipend.

---

13. These special expenses are called Impairment Related Work Expenses, or IRWE's.

CHAPTER 8

TERMINATION OF THE TRUST

No trust can last forever, and eventually every trust must end. But before the Special Needs Trust ends, the trust business must be concluded, debts and taxes paid, and accounts settled. This section explains what the trustee must do to conclude the trust in an orderly and efficient manner, while resolving potentially competing claims to the trust's assets from the beneficiary's relatives, the Medicaid program, and taxing authorities. Concluding the trust and paying final expenses poses special challenges to the trustee because if there is a shortfall, she may be personally liable to make up for that shortfall.

When does a trust end?

In most cases, the death of the lifetime beneficiary will cause the Special Needs Trust to end and require the final distribution of trust assets to the remainder beneficiaries (also called the "remaindermen"). In some cases, the trust will continue to be administered for other beneficiaries after the lifetime beneficiary has died. If that is the case, then the trustee must carefully review the trust document to determine who the new beneficiaries are and what trust standards will apply. The trustee must notify the new beneficiaries of their status, if they do not already know it.

When the trust ends, does the trustee still have authority to act?

Yes. Even if the trust instrument states that the trust ends when the lifetime beneficiary dies, that does not mean that the trustee's role has ended or that she has no authority to act. A trustee remains in office for a reasonable period of time in order to conclude the trust business and distribute the remaining assets.

What must the trustee do to properly conclude the Special Needs Trust?

In general, the trustee's activities to conclude the trust business fall into three categories: 1) paying the final expenses of the trust and perhaps the expenses of the lifetime beneficiary or his estate; 2) making a final accounting to the remainder beneficiaries; and 3) distributing any remaining assets.

Before making payments, the trustee must understand how to prioritize among the claims and debts that may be brought to her for payment. For guidance, the trustee should look to the language of the trust document and also to general principles that govern the payment of trust obligations. At this stage, the trustee would be wise to seek the advice of counsel as to which obligations to pay and when.

The practical consequence of making the wrong payment is that the trustee may be required to pay out of her personal assets any person or entity that claims it was not properly paid from the trust.

Which trust expenses should the trustee pay?

Since each trust is different, the trustee must carefully review the trust document for instructions as to which expenses to pay. However, the trustee must also consider other obligations imposed by law that may not be explicitly described in the trust instrument. What follows is a list of the expenses the trustee must consider. The difficult decision of which obligations to pay first, particularly if the trust may not have enough funds left to pay all of the expenses, should be made carefully and—ideally—with the advice of experienced counsel.

Debts of the Trust

Trust debts may include expenses incurred for case management services for the beneficiary, investment advice, legal advice, tax preparation, and so forth, that remain unpaid when the beneficiary dies. The trustee may use trust funds to pay these kinds of trust debts, even if the trust does not specifically authorize them. As with all distributions, the trustee should act reasonably and not pay exorbitant or undocumented claims.

Administrative Costs

The trustee should pay the reasonable fees for the services of professionals (accountants, tax preparers, and lawyers) engaged by the trustee to help conclude the trust business. The trustee is also entitled to pay herself a reasonable fee for her services to conclude the trust. However, it is necessary to distinguish between trustee fees for services provided to conclude the trust and unpaid fees that the trustee should have received for services rendered *before* the beneficiary's death. The trustee's right to pay herself such pre-death fees could be challenged by the state Medicaid agency (if the trustee is dealing with that agency) or by unhappy beneficiaries. This problem is discussed in the "Trustee Fees" section (Chapter 10) and also in the "Medicaid" section of this chapter.

Income Taxes

The trustee must file final federal and state income tax returns (fiduciary returns) for the trust. These tax returns will cover the period from the end of the previous tax year (for most trusts, December 31) until all of the trust bank accounts are closed and cease to generate any earnings. On the final federal tax return, all income (and losses) can be passed through the trust and taxed directly to the beneficiaries, who will report the income and losses on their personal tax returns. Thus, the trust itself will not be required not pay any federal tax on its final return. (This is the case even if in prior tax years the trust paid its own taxes on its earnings.)

The rules are different in Massachusetts, however, because in that state, even on the final return, all income is taxed to the trust and not to the beneficiaries. The rules in other states may be different. Thus, the trustee should maintain sufficient funds to pay any final taxes.

In addition to the final fiduciary tax returns, which are the direct responsibility of the trustee, the trustee should assist the legal representative of the beneficiary's estate to prepare a final income tax return for the beneficiary, and, if applicable, an estate tax return.

Estate Taxes

In some cases, the assets of a Special Needs Trust will be included in the estate of the beneficiary for estate tax purposes. Whether the trust assets will be included in the beneficiary's taxable estate depends in part on whether the Special

Needs Trust is a self-settled trust or a third-party trust (see Chapter 1). Most self-settled trusts will be included in the beneficiary's taxable estate at his death. Whether a third-party trust will be included in the beneficiary's taxable estate depends on the terms of the trust and what rights, if any, the beneficiary had to control the trust property.

If the trust is included in the beneficiary's taxable estate, then all of the trust assets, including all bank accounts, investments, real estate, and any other assets the trust owns, must be included. In the case of an annuity, the present value of the future payments to be made from the annuity is included. If a significant amount of future guaranteed payments remain outstanding at the beneficiary's death, then the present value of those payments could be substantial.

Estate taxes may not be an issue for many Special Needs Trusts, because the threshold for federal estate taxes is $950,000 in 2005 (rising to $1,000,000 in 2006). At the time this manual was published in 2005, the Massachusetts estate tax threshold is $950,000 (rising to $1,000,000 in 2006). If there is any question whether a state or federal estate tax applies, the trustee and the representative of the beneficiary's estate should consult a qualified CPA (certified public accountant) or tax attorney.

The Beneficiary's Personal Debts

The lifetime beneficiary may have outstanding charges in his own name, such as utility bills, unpaid rent, medical expenses, and so forth. If the beneficiary's personal funds (such as personal checking or savings account) are not sufficient to pay these expenses, then the trustee may be asked to do so.

The trustee may pay the beneficiary's personal debts if the trust document specifically authorizes her to do so. Problems may arise, however, if the remaining assets are not sufficient to pay both all of the beneficiary's creditors and the trust debts. The safest approach is to notify all parties who are potentially entitled to receive the trust property—including the remainder beneficiaries—and try to obtain their consent before making any payments.

If the trustee is still uncertain as how to proceed, she should discuss this situation with qualified counsel.

Funeral Expenses

Funeral expenses are generally considered a high priority obligation of a person's estate, so the trustee will very likely be permitted to pay funeral expenses if there are sufficient assets in the trust to do so. First, however, the trustee should investigate whether other resources are available to pay for these costs (a life insurance policy, for example). If the funeral arrangements have been pre-paid or if funds had been set aside for this purpose, then the earmarked funds or pre-arranged contract should be used before any trust funds are spent.

If there are not sufficient assets in the trust to pay both the funeral expenses and all of the creditors, then the trustee should be cautious about paying for funeral costs, especially if there is a potential Medicaid claim. The relationship between state Medicaid claims and other debts of the beneficiary is discussed later in this chapter.

Medicaid Reimbursement

In some cases, the trustee must use the trust assets to repay the state for Medicaid benefits that the lifetime beneficiary received. (Note, however, that SSI benefits do not have to be repaid.) Also, it is important to note that not every special needs trust involves government "payback." This is usually only a requirement if the disabled beneficiary placed his own assets in the trust in order to qualify for SSI. (In other words, the trust was "self-settled.") If the trust was funded by a third party—such as a parent leaving an inheritance to a disabled child—then government reimbursement is not usually required. This is discussed in detail in Chapter One.

How can the trustee find out how much is owed for Medicaid costs?

In Massachusetts, the trustee can find out how much is owed for Medicaid costs from the Estate Recovery Unit of the Division of Medical Assistance (DMA). The trustee may also obtain the information from the personal representative (executor or administrator) of the beneficiary's estate. For example, in Massachusetts the personal representative of the estate must notify the DMA that the beneficiary has died. This notice then prompts the DMA to file a Notice of

Claim, showing the total amount the DMA claims for the benefits provided to the beneficiary.

The trustee should ask the DMA for an itemized statement of medical charges, which the DMA will provide upon request. The trustee should carefully review the DMA's statement to confirm that the amounts charged for the services appear to be reasonably accurate. The dates of service can be important too. For example, if the Special Needs Trust was funded with the net proceeds of a personal injury settlement, then the state will often have been reimbursed before any funds were transferred to the Special Needs Trust. In this case, it is important to make sure that the repayment that the state is seeking does not include charges that were already paid back before the trust was funded. In other words, the trustee must be sure that the state is not erroneously seeking a double payment.

The situation is different, however, if the state was never reimbursed. An example would be if the beneficiary had inherited the property in the Special Needs Trust. In that case, the state is entitled to be paid back for all the Medicaid benefits it provided, including Medicaid benefits paid before the trust was created or funded.

Can the Medicaid bill be challenged?

Yes. If the trustee disagrees with a particular item on the state's bill, then that item can be challenged. The time and effort required to do so, however, may be daunting. The trustee will have to locate the medical provider to obtain the old billing data, and then compare that information to the DMA records. Unless the size of the suspected error is substantial, few cases will be worth the effort of a challenge.

What happens if there are not enough funds to pay the Medicaid costs?

In some cases, the state's claim for Medicaid reimbursement is so large that the trustee cannot pay the funeral expenses, administrative expenses or beneficiary's debts because there are not enough funds left in the trust to meet all of these competing demands. As explained earlier, the trustee must proceed with caution to avoid making herself or the other trust beneficiaries personally liable for any shortfall that cannot be paid to the creditors, including the state Medicaid agency.

Currently, in Massachusetts, there are no laws or regulations specifying which expenses, if any, have priority over the reimbursement to Medicaid. Attorneys who have dealt with the DMA on this issue, however, report that the DMA appears to have an internal policy that governs this situation. Unfortunately, the DMA has not published that policy nor has it released any written memorandum that attorneys or the general public may use for guidance. And, of course, the DMA's current practice, because it is an informal one, could change at any time.

Reportedly, the DMA's current internal policy allows the trustee to pay for certain items before paying the state's Medicaid bill. The permitted items include taxes, reasonable funeral costs, and reasonable administrative fees to conclude the trust business. According to the DMA's policy, "taxes" include both personal taxes of the beneficiary and fiduciary taxes owed to the state and federal governments. "Funeral expenses" may include funeral and burial costs, cemetery expenses, and a headstone or other grave marker. The DMA would probably not approve the cost of a reception, such as a catered luncheon, after the funeral. The DMA allows the trustee to pay for reasonable administrative costs to conclude the trust business, such as the services of the trustee, attorney, or an accountant.

The operative word here is "reasonable." The DMA does not necessarily approve every funeral or administrative expense that the trustee submits. Not surprisingly, the DMA and the trustee may not agree about which expenses should be paid. Attorneys who have dealt with the DMA on this issue report that in some cases the DMA has set a cap on funeral expenses, even though the actual costs of the funeral exceeded the "approved" amount. In other instances, the DMA may limit the amount that the attorney or trustee can charge for services to conclude the trust business. The trustee may have to negotiate a mutually acceptable resolution.

With respect to the trustee fees, the DMA allows the trustee to pay herself a reasonable fee to conclude the trust business. A problem can arise, however, if the trustee wants to pay herself or a predecessor trustee for services provided before the lifetime beneficiary died. Reportedly, the DMA will not allow these charges. Thus, if for any reason the trustee had failed to pay herself while the beneficiary was alive and then attempts to pay herself after the beneficiary's death, she will find herself in line behind the state Medicaid agency and quite likely not paid for her services. To avoid this result, the trustee should consistently pay herself on a regular basis.

If there is a deficit and the Medicaid claim cannot be paid in full, then the trustee should address this problem with the DMA before making any final payments for any other expenses. A number of attorneys suggest that the trustee prepare an itemized list of the payments the trustee proposes to make and request that DMA review and approve of the proposed payments. If the DMA agrees to the proposal, the trustee would pay the Medicaid bill in exchange for a written Release from the DMA. The Release should specifically state that the state's claim has been satisfied; that the state will not later challenge any of the agreed expenditures; and that the trustee and remainder beneficiaries will not be held personally liable for any shortfall.

Medicaid reimbursement is a complicated problem. If it appears that the Medicaid claim could exceed the trust assets, the trustee should consult an attorney before paying any expenses or claims. Consulting an attorney experienced in this area of law will allow the trustee to know the current practices in a particular state before she proceeds to make payments that may be questioned later.

What is the final account?

Most Special Needs Trusts contain a provision that requires the trustee to prepare and distribute a final account when the trust is concluded. Even if the trust instrument does not explicitly require a final account, the trustee has a duty under general fiduciary principles to render a final account. The trustee should review the trust instrument to determine to whom the final account must be provided. A description of the accounting procedure is located in the "Trust Management" section (Chapter 10) of this handbook.

The final account must cover the period from the end of the previous account through the time the trust is concluded. In addition to showing all income to and disbursements from the trust, the final account must also show the exact amount of money or property each remainder beneficiary will receive. Unlike earlier accounts, the final account must have a zero balance. A sample Final Account is contained in the Appendix.

In addition to providing a final account to the remainder beneficiaries, the trustee should obtain their written assent to that account. This is for the trustee's own protection, because any beneficiary who has previously assented to the account cannot later challenge the trustee on any particular item.

For added protection, some attorneys even recommend that the trustee have each remainder beneficiary assent to the final account *before* a final distribution will be made to them as remaindermen. This will prevent the trustee from finding herself in a situation where the trust assets are gone, but she must defend her account and risk personally paying for any error. If the trustee wants to proceed as suggested, then she must send each beneficiary her proposed account and an "Assent" form. When she receives the signed Assent forms back from all remaindermen, then at that time the trust bank accounts can be closed and the assets distributed. Two sample Assent forms are included in the Appendix.

Should the trustee make partial distributions?

Sometimes there can be a delay in making the final distribution of the trust assets, and so the trustee may be asked to make a partial distribution before the entire trust business has been concluded. The trustee has the discretion, but not the obligation, to make partial distributions. No beneficiary can require the trustee to make a partial distribution. As with payments of expenses and creditors' claims, the trustee should proceed with utmost caution. If the trustee makes a distribution to a beneficiary and, as a result, the trust lacks sufficient funds to pay its liabilities, the trustee may be personally liable for any outstanding obligations. In other words, if the trust assets are gone but there are still debts outstanding, the trustee may have to pay the debts out of her personal assets.

Before making any distributions, the trustee must consider both the amount of any trust obligations and the nature of such obligations. For example, a trust with $250,000 in assets may undergo an IRS audit. If the amount at issue is no more than $10,000 of taxes due, including interest and penalties, and all other obligations have been paid, then the trustee might reasonably make preliminary distributions to the beneficiaries totaling $225,000 (reserving $50,000 to cover the anticipated tax obligation and professional fees). If, however, the tax obligation is not clear and could be a considerable amount with penalties and interest, the trustee would be ill advised to make any partial distributions.

How does the trust make its final distributions?

After all the obligations have been paid and the beneficiaries have assented to the trustee's final account, then the trustee can make the final distributions and conclude the trust.

Most trust instruments permit the trustee to distribute the trust assets in cash, or "in kind." In this context, the term "in kind" means the equivalent of cash.

The type of transaction required to distribute the trust property depends on the type of property that the trust owns. Consider for example a trust portfolio that consists of cash, mutual funds, bonds, and real estate. The cash accounts, such as bank accounts, would be distributed by writing checks or other bank drafts. The mutual funds or bonds can be distributed either: 1) by cashing in the investment and converting it to cash, or 2) by assigning the property to new accounts opened in the name of each beneficiary. It is advisable for the trustee to obtain written authorization from the beneficiary before the trustee sells stocks, bonds, or mutual funds because a sale could have adverse tax consequences. A sale could also subject the trustee to criticism from a beneficiary who in retrospect decides that selling the asset was not a good idea.

Real estate is distributed by a deed from the trustee conveying the property to the remainder beneficiaries in whatever shares the trust instrument specifies. The trustee should get the advice of an attorney and/or CPA as to the mechanics and the potential tax consequences of the method by which the trustee distributes the assets to the beneficiaries.

How soon after the death of the lifetime beneficiary must the trust be concluded?

There is no specific length of time that the trust must remain open after the beneficiary's death. Some small trusts may be closed within a few weeks. Larger trusts, or trusts with competing claims for payments, could remain open for a year or more, depending on the complexity of the trust affairs and other circumstances that could delay the completion of the final account and the final trust distributions.

CHAPTER 9

TAXES

Tax issues for Special Needs Trusts can be confounding if not downright "taxing" for the trustee. One reason is that the IRS has its own definition of terms, which may be different from those the Social Security Administration uses. For example, the term "grantor" has a different meaning depending on whether one is dealing with the IRS or the Social Security Administration. Also, the term "income" for federal tax purposes is much broader than "income" for SSI purposes. This can cause headaches for the trustee who must deal with the income sensitive SSI program.

The following discussion of taxes and the Special Needs Trust is intended to help the trustee navigate this complicated area. However, our observations are intended for general guidance only, and not as a substitute for expert tax advice in any specific situation. For that, the trustee should work with a tax professional who is knowledgeable about public benefits and the Special Needs Trust.

Should the trustee notify the IRS after the trust has been signed?

Yes. In most cases, a Special Needs Trust will be treated as a separate taxpayer for state and federal income tax purposes. Therefore, the trustee should notify the IRS of the trust's existence after the trust has been signed.

The trustee notifies the IRS by applying for an employer identification number (EIN)[14]. The EIN can be obtained by filing an SS-4 Form ("Application for Employer Identification Number") with the Internal Revenue Service. Also, the IRS is now issuing EIN's over the telephone (1-800-829-4933) and on-line at http://www.irs.gov. If applying by telephone, the trustee must personally place the call and provide the IRS with: 1) the name of the trust; 2) the name of the

---

14. Also called a Taxpayer Identification Number (TIN).

grantor (see below); 3) the grantor's social security number (see below); 4) the name of the trustee; 5) the trustee's address; 6) the trustee's social security number; and 7) the trustee's date of birth.

Identifying the "grantor" on the SS-4 form can be tricky because the term "grantor" has different meanings for the IRS and the Social Security Administration. For IRS purposes, the identity of the grantor depends on whether the trust is a "third party" or a "self-settled" trust.

A "third party trust" is one that is created by someone other than the disabled beneficiary and funded with that person's (or another person's) assets. An example of a third party trust is a trust established by a parent for her child with disabilities and funded with assets from the parent's estate. In that case, the situation is relatively straightforward. The parent is the "grantor" for IRS purposes and her name and social security number should be used, and not those of the beneficiary.

Some trusts are "self-settled," that is, created by the disabled beneficiary for his own benefit, and funded with his own assets. An example of a self-settled trust is one in which a person with disabilities places the proceeds of a personal injury award into a trust for his own use. The complicating factor here is that in order to comply with certain Medicaid and SSI rules as of January 1, 2000, the person creating this type of trust (who is called the "grantor" or "declarant") must be the parent, grandparent, or legal guardian of the disabled beneficiary, or a court. (This is the rule even though the trust is funded entirely with money belonging to the disabled beneficiary.) In this case, the disabled beneficiary is treated as the "grantor" for tax purposes. His name and social security number should be provided to the IRS, not the social security numbers of the parent, grandparent, or legal guardian, *even though that person may be called the "grantor" on the trust instrument.*

Should the beneficiary's Social Security Number be used on trust bank accounts?

No. Once the EIN has been assigned, it should be used on all trust bank and investment accounts and on all trust income tax returns.

Are the funds initially placed in the trust taxable?

In most cases, the trust's initial funds are not subject to any income tax. This would be true even if the funds come from the settlement of a personal injury action (although any pre-judgment or post-judgment interest would be taxable). Also, the settlement would be tax-free regardless of whether the award was paid as a lump sum or in installments through an annuity. Likewise, if the trust is funded by an inheritance, receipt of those funds by the trust would not generate a tax, although depending on the size of the estate that paid the inheritance, an estate tax might be owed. (In that case, however, any estate tax would have been paid from estate funds before the inheritance was distributed.)

If the initial funds placed in the trust were not subject to tax, is any subsequent income also exempt?

No. In most cases, a tax must be paid on the income that a trust earns. Once funds are invested, they will generate income that may take the form of interest, dividends, or capital gains. If an account is opened at a bank, then the bank will pay interest on a monthly basis. If the trustee invests some of the trust's money in bonds, then the trustees will likely receive interest payments every six months. If money is invested in stocks, dividends may be paid every three months. All of these payments constitute income and are subject to state and federal income taxes. However, some investments, such as U.S. Treasury bonds and municipal bonds are exempt from state and/or federal taxes.

Are capital gains taxed?

Yes. A capital gain is realized when an investment is sold if the sale price exceeds the purchase price. The maximum federal tax on long-term capital gains (investments held for more than 12 months) is generally 20 percent.

What is the tax rate for Special Needs Trusts?

The answer to this question is complicated. It depends, in part, on whether or not the trust is considered to be a "grantor trust" for tax purposes. If the trust is a grantor trust, then any income that the trust receives may be passed through to the beneficiary and taxed at the beneficiary's personal rate. However, if the trust is not a grantor trust, then any income will be taxed at a higher trust tax rate unless the income was distributed, in which case it may be taxed at the beneficiary's personal rate.

Most self-settled trusts are written to comply with the so-called grantor trust rules. Those rules allow the trust's ordinary income (interest and dividends, etc.) and deductions to "pass through" the trust and be taxed to the beneficiary at his personal tax rate, even if the income is retained by the trust and not distributed.

Tax-wise, grantor trusts present a favorable situation, because income tax rates for individuals are generally lower than those for trusts. For example, the federal tax for a trust in 2002 reached a maximum of 39.6 percent on any income over $8,900. However, the federal rate for an individual did not reach 39.6 percent until the individual had income of $297,300.

With regard to the tax filings, a grantor trust files its own income tax return (Federal Form 1041 and Mass. Form 2G). However, the trustee states on the Form 1041 that the return is for "information only" and that all income and deductions flow through to the beneficiary, whose name and social security number are listed on the form. The trust itself does not pay any tax. Instead, the beneficiary reports the trust income (and any deductions) on his personal tax return and pays tax at his individual rate.

A third party trust, however, is a separate taxable entity which must pay taxes at the trust rate on any income it does not distribute.[15]

From a tax perspective, a third party trust presents a disadvantageous situation because of the comparatively high trust tax rates. As with the self-settled trusts, the trust files the federal Form 1041 and Mass. Form 2G. If any of the trust's income has been paid to the beneficiary (or to another person for his benefit), then those distributions are listed on Schedule K-1, which is sent to both the IRS and the beneficiary. The trust pays tax (at the trust rate) on all undistributed income, and the beneficiary pays tax on distributed income (from the K-1) at his personal tax rate. (However, this is not the case in Massachusetts, because that state does not permit a third party trust to deduct the income it distributes. Instead, in Massachusetts, a trust must pay tax at the trust rate on all of its income, even if that income is distributed.)

---

15. This is also true for a self-settled trust that does not include the language required to make it a grantor trust for tax purposes.

Will there be a problem with SSI if trust income is reported under the beneficiary's social security number?

Sometimes a troublesome situation can occur with Social Security when trust earnings are reported to the IRS under the beneficiary's social security number. Those earnings may come to the attention of the Social Security Administration, which routinely cross-checks information with the IRS. Although the SSI recipient may have received income (on paper) for tax purposes, he has not received any income (food or shelter) for SSI purposes. Nevertheless, the Social Security Administration may erroneously believe that the recipient has received unreported income and send out a letter of inquiry, or even require the recipient to come to a face-to-face meeting.

In this situation, a proactive approach may be helpful. Some trustees routinely provide Social Security with copies of the annual trust tax return, the beneficiary's personal income tax return, and a letter explaining that although the beneficiary may have received "income" (on paper) for income tax purposes, he has not received "income" (cash, food or shelter) for SSI purposes. So far, this seems to work satisfactorily to avert a crisis.

Is it possible to reduce the amount of income taxes the Special Needs Trust must pay?

If the high rate of trust income taxes is a concern, then one strategy to reduce taxes might be to purchase tax-free investments such as municipal bonds.

Another strategy might be to make distributions from the trust to the beneficiary, since the trust does not have to pay tax on any money it distributes. However, before proceeding, the trustee must carefully consider the impact that any distributions would have on the beneficiary's government benefits.

As explained throughout this manual, if the beneficiary receives SSI, then any cash distribution in excess of $20 per month will reduce and could potentially eliminate the SSI benefit. Therefore, it is likely that any potential tax savings would be more than offset by a reduction in SSI. However, since trust distributions to third parties for goods and services provided to the recipient will not affect SSI (so long as the distributions are not food or shelter items)[16], then this type of distribution should be considered, if that is consistent with the overall trust objectives and the welfare of the beneficiary.

---

16. For example, payments to a third party for medical care or a vacation package would not affect the SSI benefit.

CHAPTER 10

TRUST MANAGEMENT

Trustee Provisions

Where are the rules concerning the appointment and removal of trustees found?

Most trust instruments have provisions that govern the appointment and removal of trustees. Specifically, those provisions cover matters such as: (1) who will serve as the initial trustee; (2) who has the right to appoint a successor trustee; (3) the qualifications, if any, that any successor trustee must meet; (4) who has the right to remove a trustee; and (5) the standard, if any, that must be applied to remove a trustee. Any prospective trustee should review these provisions carefully.

How is the initial trustee identified?

The trust instrument should identify the initial trustee. The trustee might be an individual or an institution, such as a bank. When two or more persons or institutions act as Trustees, they are called Co-Trustees.

How does a trustee accept her appointment?

The initial trustee could sign the actual trust instrument, thereby accepting his or her appointment. Alternatively, the initial trustee could sign a separate document called an "Acceptance." A sample Acceptance is located in the Appendix.

In some cases, a court or a third party may have to approve a trustee's appointment. This type of review requirement should appear in the trust instrument. If court or third-party review is required, then the prospective trustee should ask for a written statement confirming that the review has taken place and that her appointment has been approved.

A prospective trustee should not act until the formal appointment process has been completed.

What are successor trustees, and how are they chosen?

A successor trustee is one who serves after the initial trustee.

Most trusts identify the successor trustee or trustees, or provide a method for choosing one.

A successor trustee should sign an Acceptance. A sample Acceptance is included in the Appendix.

What happens if a successor trustee named in the trust does not want to serve?

The individual who declines to serve as trustee must sign a "Declination." A sample Declination is located in the Appendix.

How does a trustee resign?

Most Special Needs Trusts have a procedure for a trustee to resign. Typically, this will require the resigning trustee to provide written notice to the beneficiary and to the person(s) who have the right to appoint and remove trustees. A sample Resignation form is included with the Appendix.

If a court is supervising the trust, then court approval may be required for the trustee to resign. A court will probably not accept a resignation unless all of the outgoing trustee's accounts have been filed and a successor trustee is ready to take over from the resigning trustee.

Even if a court is not involved, a resigning trustee should not assume that she is "off the hook" simply by delivering the required notice. The resigning trustee may likely remain responsible for anything that happens to the trust property until a successor trustee takes possession. And, of course, the resigning trustee will remain liable for her actions during her trusteeship.

What if the trustee is not doing her job and must be fired?

Most Special Needs Trusts contain provisions that describe how a trustee can be fired. For example, some trusts might require court approval before a trustee can be fired, while others may simply authorize a third person to fire the trustee. Sometimes a trust may limit the number of times trustees can be fired in any given period.

The standard for removing trustees can also vary from trust to trust. Some trusts state that a trustee can only be removed for reasonable cause, while other trusts may allow a trustee to be removed at any time and for any reason.

Should the beneficiary also serve as trustee?

No. One of the goals of the Special Needs Trust is to prevent the trust from being counted as an asset for most government benefit programs. This is difficult, if not impossible, to accomplish if the disabled beneficiary is also the trustee. If the trust document names the disabled beneficiary as an initial trustee, then the beneficiary should immediately resign and make arrangements for the prompt appointment of a successor trustee.

What is an independent trustee?

An independent trustee is one who has no beneficial interest in the trust property. This means that the independent trustee can never be eligible to receive any trust property (other than her reasonable trustee's fee). Accordingly, neither the beneficiary nor any member of his family could qualify as an independent trustee.

When is it appropriate to have an independent trustee?

There are often sound public benefits reasons, as well as "family dynamics" reasons, for a Special Needs Trust to have an independent trustee.

First, while various government programs might not have any explicit require-ment that the trustee be independent, it can be an implied requirement. Some government programs do not count the trust property as a resource on the theory that the beneficiary does not have any control over the trust property. This argu-ment is difficult to make, for example, if the beneficiary is a minor child and the trustee is the child's parent.

Second, an independent trustee may be able to avoid the conflicts of interest that can arise for a family trustee. For example, an independent trustee may be in a much better position to distinguish between the family's needs and the benefi-ciary's needs. An independent trustee can also serve as an objective voice in a sit-uation that can easily become emotionally charged.

Bonds

What is a surety bond, and must the trustee post one?

A surety bond is insurance that protects the beneficiary if the trustee misman-ages or misappropriates the trust property. Whether the trustee must post a bond, and if so, what type, is usually stated in the trust instrument. Some Special Needs Trusts excuse a trustee who is a relative of the beneficiary from giving bond, but require a professional or corporate trustee to post a bond. In this context, a pro-fessional trustee usually means an attorney, accountant, or other business profes-sional who is not related by blood to the beneficiary. A bank or other financial institution is an example of a corporate trustee.

Professional trustees such as accountants and attorneys often have malpractice or fidelity insurance to cover their trust management activities. Institutional trustees such as banks have a fidelity insurance policy that provides coverage equivalent to a corporate bond. In each instance, the trustee should review the policy to make sure that the coverage is adequate.

If the trustee must obtain a corporate bond, then who should for pay the pre-mium? This point may be negotiated between the trustee and the person(s) hav-ing the right to appoint and remove trustees. If the insurance duplicates coverage that the trustee already carries at his own expense, then the trust will likely be asked to pay the premium from trust assets.

Bank Accounts, Check Writing, and Contracts

What does the trustee need to know about setting up a bank account, writing checks, and signing her name?

When a bank or investment account has been opened and trust funds have been deposited into that account, then it is said that the trust has become "funded." Until that occurs, the trust is "unfunded."

Each bank has its own requirements for opening trust accounts. In general, most banks require the trustee to provide the bank with a photocopy of the trust instrument, the employer identification number (EIN) that will be used on the account, and funds to open the account.[17] The bank will also require at least one form of personal identification from the trustee, such as a driver's license.

The title of the bank account usually includes both the name of the trust and the trustee's name, for example, "Jane Doe, Trustee of The John Doe Special Needs Trust." It is not necessary for the trustee's name to appear on the checks; however, merchants may more readily accept payment from the trustee if her name appears on the check.

The trustee should sign her name by writing her customary signature. It is not necessary to write the word "trustee" after her name.

However, if the trustee signs a contract or other legal document, such as a credit card application or apartment lease, then she should go one step further. In that situation, wherever her name appears, the trustee should write the words "Jane Doe, as Trustee of the John Doe Special Needs Trust, and not individually". Then, the trustee should sign her name "Jane Doe, Trustee." This will make it clear that the trustee is entering into the contract only in her fiduciary capacity, and not personally. This will protect the trustee by putting the merchant or lender on notice that he can look only to trust assets, not the trustee's personal assets, to satisfy any claims.

---

17. The EIN is discussed in the "Taxes" section (Chapter 9) of this manual.

Record Keeping

What records must the trustee maintain, and for how long?

The trustee must keep detailed records of the trust's activities. Bank statements, cancelled checks, check registers, and brokerage statements should be organized and kept with the trust records. To the extent possible, invoices and receipts should be retained for all purchases. Some trustees prepare and retain notes on any large disbursements. These contemporaneous notes can provide an indication as to why the trustee thought the particular disbursement was appropriate. The notes might include a summary of discussions between the trustee and the beneficiary or others concerning the disbursement.

In short, there should be a paper trail for every dollar that comes in or goes out of the trust. Even if a trustee is doing a good job investing the trust property, the trustee will be exposed to risk if her records are inadequate. A trustee can never know when an unhappy beneficiary or a "concerned" third party may complain about the trust management.

Records should be kept stored and available for review by the beneficiaries for as long as possible. If the trust is large and the records are voluminous, the trustee could consider renting storage space. The cost of storage may be charged to the trust.

Trustee Fees

May the trustee charge a fee?

Yes. A basic principle of trust law is that the trustee is entitled to be paid for her services. Many Special Needs Trusts specifically state that the trustee will receive reasonable compensation. However, in Massachusetts, even if the trust document does not contain a specific provision to that effect, a trustee is still entitled to be paid.

How much do trustees charge?

In Massachusetts, there are no standard fees for trustees. Fees may be flat (i.e., $5,000 per year), based on the size of the trust, or charged hourly. Also, the rates vary depending on whether the trustee is an institutional or professional trustee, or a non-professional trustee, such as a family member.

Institutional and Professional Trustees: An institutional trustee (such as a bank) and some professional trustees often set their annual fee based on the size of the trust. The following is a sample fee schedule:

> 1.0 percent (1.0%) of the trust's market value for amounts up to $500,000.
> .80 percent (.80%) of the trust's market value for amounts ranging from $500,001 up to $1,000,000.
> .30 percent (.30%) of the trust's market value for amounts ranging from $1,000,001 up to $5,000,000.
> .10 percent (.10%) of the trust's market value for amounts over $5,000.000.
> Plus 6 percent (6.0%) of the income earned.
> Minimum annual fee is $2,200.

The scope of services included in an institutional or professional trustee's fee schedule will vary from trust to trust. Some trustees might charge more if an outside investment advisor or an accountant is hired. Other trustees might charge more if they are required to post a bond. A trustee might charge an additional fee if time has to be spent on SSI or Medicaid matters. Lastly, if the trustee is also providing legal services, then the legal fees may be charged in addition to the trustee's normal fees.

Non-Professional Trustees: Most non-professional trustees, including family members, charge an hourly rate for services. The trustee's hourly rate depends on her skills and background. For example, a trustee with a financial services background may charge an hourly rate commensurate with her skills, such as $50 to $75 per hour, while a trustee without financial or even bookkeeping skills might only charge $10 to $15 per hour. If the trustee pays herself an hourly rate, she may have the trust pay any additional administrative costs, such as accounting and attorney's fees.

What time and billing records should the trustee maintain?

The trustee should maintain a contemporaneous written record of all services she provides for the trust. Some trustees find it convenient to maintain a logbook, in which they write down the date, nature of the service, and time spent. Additionally, if the trustee reimburses herself for any expenses, she must keep receipts for all these disbursements. The trustee's records should be kept until the trust has been concluded and the remainder beneficiaries (including the state, if applicable) have approved the trustee's final account.

How often are trustees paid?

Most non-professional trustees are paid at least annually. Many institutional and professional trustees bill quarterly or even monthly for their services.

What happens if the trustee neglects to pay herself?

After a trustee has established how much she will charge, she should pay herself consistently on a regular basis. This may prevent potential problems with the beneficiary's relatives or the state Medicaid agency when the trust ends.

Some trustees, however, are reluctant to pay themselves anything while the beneficiary is alive. This is especially true if the trustee is a close relative of the disabled beneficiary. These trustees are uncomfortable taking money from a family member with a disability who might need that money in the future. Their plan is to pay themselves after the beneficiary has died, if there are sufficient funds left in the trust to do so.

This way of thinking, while laudable, may cause substantial problems for the trustee when the trust ends. One possible difficulty could come from the remainder beneficiaries. (The remainder beneficiaries are the individuals—usually members of the disabled beneficiary's family, and sometimes charities—who will receive the remaining trust funds when the disabled beneficiary dies and the trust ends.) For example, if the trustee has not paid herself anything while the beneficiary was alive and then on his death pays herself for, say, the past ten years, the remainder beneficiaries might balk at approving her fee. However, as long as the trustee's rate of payment is reasonable and the services were actually performed, the trustee would most likely prevail in a fee dispute, because a trustee is entitled to be paid (even belatedly) for her services.

Nevertheless, a prudent trustee should avoid putting herself in a position where her fee can be questioned. A better practice is for the trustee to pay herself regularly every year, and then list her fee on her annual Account, which she provides to all of the remainder beneficiaries. (A description of the trust Accounting procedures is contained in the "Trustee's Duties" section of this chapter.) That way, if the remainder beneficiaries have had full disclosure about the trustee's fees on an annual basis, they will not be able at a later date to challenge the reasonableness of her fee.

The trustee who defers paying herself could also face a significant problem with the state Medicaid agency. The trustee might be dealing with that agency if the trust contains a so-called Medicaid payback provision. (A Medicaid payback provision states that when the lifetime beneficiary dies, any assets that remain in the trust must be used to repay the state for medical benefits provided to the lifetime beneficiary.) In that case, the state Medicaid agency will assert a claim on the trust assets for the total cost of the beneficiary's medical services. If the cost of those services is more than the remaining trust assets, then the state's claim might have priority over the unpaid trustee's fee. That being the case, the trustee may not receive anything for her services. The problem of Medicaid recovery and unpaid trustee fees is discussed in detail the "Termination of the Trust" section (Chapter 8).

Loans

Should the trustee make loans?

Sometimes family members or friends of the beneficiary may ask to borrow money from the trust. Some trustees report being besieged by loan demands from family members who learn that the beneficiary has "come into some money."

Whether or not trust funds should be loaned can be a difficult decision for the trustee. She may understandably feel generous toward those who care for the disabled beneficiary. The beneficiary may even encourage her to loan his money. However, she must remain keenly aware of her fiduciary duty to safeguard the trust property for the beneficiary.

In considering a loan request, the trustee should first carefully review the trust document to determine if she has authority to make loans. This authority is usually contained in the "trustee's powers" section of the trust instrument. Some trust documents confer broad loan powers that permit the trustee to use trust property to make personal, unsecured loans for any purpose that the trustee deems worthwhile.

Next, if the trustee determines that she *can* loan trust funds, *should* she do so?

Here the trustee must weigh a number of factors. Certainly the purpose of the loan must be considered. For example, a loan to purchase a vehicle to transport the beneficiary may be prudent, whereas a loan to finance the family's start-up business should probably be rejected. Also, the identity of the borrower is a factor. A close family member who takes care of the beneficiary may be acceptable, whereas a newfound friend should be passed over. The credit-worthiness of the borrower must also be taken into account. A prospective borrower who is struggling financially or has failed to repay other obligations is not a good loan candidate. Lastly, and most importantly, the relative size of the trust fund and the amount of the proposed loan are considerations. A comparatively small loan from a sizeable trust fund may be acceptable, whereas a loan that consumes a substantial portion of the trust assets would be imprudent and therefore should probably be rejected.

The trustee must always consider that the loan might not be repaid in a timely manner. In that event, is the trustee willing to do "whatever it takes" to collect the loan, including take legal action? Even a court judgment is no guarantee that the loan proceeds can be recovered. Furthermore, the trustee's belated attempt to correct her error may not be worth the expense and ill will engendered by litigation.

If the trustee approves a loan, then the terms of the loan should be in writing. The trustee should have an attorney prepare the necessary promissory note and other appropriate loan documents.

For larger loans, the trustee should ask the borrower to pledge an asset as security. Typically, the borrower's house or motor vehicle can be used as collateral. An attorney can prepare the necessary documents, including security instruments, such as a mortgage, and arrange for their recording.

Trustee Duties

What are the trustee's duties?

Many trustees are surprised to learn that they have duties and responsibilities that are not usually contained or described in the trust instrument. Those obligations may vary from state to state, and which state's laws and practices will govern depends on the particular trust. Most trust instruments specifically provide that they will be governed by the laws of the state in which the trust was created, or where the trust property is located. Thus, to familiarize herself with her duties, the trustee must read the trust document carefully to determine which state's laws will govern, and then consult a local attorney for direction in this area.

In addition to consulting with an attorney, a trustee should consider purchasing a reference work on trust administration, such as *Loring: A Trustee's Handbook*[18]. First published in 1898 and most recently revised in 2002 by Professor Charles E. Rounds, Jr., *Loring* is an excellent one-volume reference book that addresses most trust issues.

With respect to a trustee's duties, most legal authorities, including *Loring*, identify several primary duties, which are summarized below.

A. *The Duty to Be Generally Prudent.*

The duty to be prudent arises from an 1830 Massachusetts court case, "Harvard College v. Amory," in which the court stated that an amateur (non-professional) trustee must exercise "such care and skill as a man of ordinary prudence would exercise in dealing with his own property."[19] The idea that a trustee's actions should be compared to those of a "prudent" person is now widely accepted. In fact, in matters of financial management, many states, including Massachusetts, have adopted a Prudent Investor Act (discussed in the "Investments" section of this chapter). The question that a trustee should pose to herself should be, "What would a prudent person do in the same circumstances?" A trustee should not exercise extreme risk or caution. Nor is she expected to have extraordinary skills. Rather, she should generally act in a reasonable manner given the facts with which she is faced.

---

18. Rounds, Charles E., Jr., *Loring: A Trustee's Handbook*. Aspen Publishers, Inc., 2002.
19. 26 Mass. (9 Pick.) 446,461.

B. *The Duty to Carry Out the Terms Of the Trust.*

The trustee has a paramount duty to carry out the intentions of the Grantor as expressed in the trust document. The trustee must therefore carefully read the trust document to determine what the Grantor intended. How did the Grantor want the trust property to be used? What guidelines, if any, did the Grantor provide concerning trust distributions? According to *Loring*, the wishes of the beneficiary must *always* be subordinate to those of the Grantor. (§ 6.1.2, p. 171)

Discerning the Grantor's intent can sometimes be difficult for the trustee of a Special Needs Trust. A common situation that can arise involves a disabled beneficiary who receives SSI but needs adequate housing, which the Trustee has sufficient funds to pay for, but only at the cost of reducing the beneficiary's SSI benefit.[20] The trust instrument may contain mutually contradictory instructions, directing trustee both to "supplement but not supplant public benefits" and to "use the trust property in ways that will best help the beneficiary lead a comfortable and fulfilling life," or words to that effect. Both instructions may not be achievable.

Thus, the trustee must look for clues in the entire document, striving to discern the Grantor's overall intent. In most cases, especially if the Grantor is the beneficiary's parent, the primary goal of the trust will be the beneficiary's, health, happiness, and well-being. The trustee can usually find adequate support for her decision to purchase comfortable housing, even if it causes a modest reduction in public benefits.

C. *Duty to Be Loyal to the Trust.*

The duty of loyalty is also called the "fiduciary duty". According to *Loring*, "A trustee is under a duty to act solely in the interest of the beneficiaries as to matters that directly and indirectly involve the trust property.

This duty arises from the trust relationship rather than from any specific provision in the trust instrument. According to *Loring*, the duty of loyalty is "the bedrock of the trust relationship; it is a duty of undivided loyalty." (§ 6.1.3, p. 172)

---

20. As explained in the "Housing" section (Chapter 3), in most states, the trustee's payment of the beneficiary's housing costs will cause SSI to be reduced.

It is this duty of loyalty that prohibits the trustee from entering into most types of personal business transactions with the trust. These transactions are called "self-dealing" (i.e., the trustee, acting in her fiduciary capacity, enters into a transaction with herself in her individual capacity). Some examples of self-dealing are the trustee borrowing money from the trust, lending money to the trust, lending trust assets to her family or friends, buying property from the trust, or selling property to the trust.

The basic rule is that a trustee must not allow her interests to compete with the trust's or the beneficiaries' interests. A trustee cannot avoid a conflict of interest if she engages in a self-dealing transaction. Even if there is a decent rationalization for the transaction and the proposed terms are by all objective standards fair, reasonable, and beneficial for the trust, most trust experts would agree that the trustee should not proceed with the deal. Finding a neutral third party to represent the trust for purposes of the proposed transaction is not the answer. The only option is for the trustee to resign and then go forward in her individual capacity. Even then, however, the former trustee may open herself up to charges that she has abused her fiduciary position.

An exception to the self-dealing rule concerns payment of fiduciary fees. A trustee is entitled to take money from the trust assets for her fee for fiduciary services. This is an inherent conflict, but, according to *Loring*, it is nevertheless permitted since it would be unreasonable to expect a trustee to serve without compensation. (§6.1.3, p. 174)

The duty of loyalty can be difficult to maintain if the trustee is the parent of the minor disabled beneficiary. Inevitably, conflicts of interest will arise because the needs of the beneficiary and parent are so closely intertwined. This is one reason it is often recommended that a Special Needs Trust have an independent trustee who can sort through issues such as transportation, housing, and family vacations.

D. *The Duty to Give Personal Attention to the Affairs of the Trust*.

A trustee may not delegate overall responsibility for a trust's management to another person. Ultimately, it is the trustee's responsibility to make sure that the trust is operating properly.

However, there are several areas in which a trustee can delegate specific duties. For example, the trustee may hire an investment advisor for advice on financial investments or an accountant to assure that the annual tax returns are accurate and filed on time. The trustee may hire a bank to act as custodian of the trust's investments.

In general, a trustee should seek outside assistance when confronted with matters with which she is not familiar. However, the trustee has a responsibility to make sure that the persons she chooses for assistance are well qualified. Also, even after delegating responsibilities, the trustee should always review any major decisions affecting the trust. For the most part, this includes decisions on investments and disbursements.

E. *The Duty to Account to the Beneficiary.*

An account (or accounting) is a summary of trust activities for a specific period of time, usually a year. The account must include: (a) all income that the trustee received; (b) all expenses that the trustee paid; and (c) the balance of the property remaining in the trust at the end of the period. Also, the account should include a snapshot of the market value of the trust assets on the last day of the accounting period.

A three-schedule account should be sufficient for most small trusts. A sample three-schedule account is included with the Appendix. Some professional trustees prepare five-schedule accounts. A sample five-schedule account is also included in the Appendix.

How often the trustee must provide an account may be specified in the trust instrument. If the trust does not state the frequency, then an account should be prepared annually. Some trustees provide a summary of activities to the beneficiaries on a quarterly or even monthly basis. They recognize that the simplest way to keep a beneficiary satisfied on a long-term basis is to provide him with frequent detailed reports of the trust activities. The goal is simple: no surprises.

In addition to satisfying the beneficiary, a proper account may provide some protection to the trustee as well. Most trust instruments prohibit the beneficiary from challenging the trustee on a particular matter (such as a specific distribution from the trust) after a certain period of time has passed. A common provision gives the beneficiary (or the beneficiary's legal guardian) a 90-day period to object to an account. If, after 90 days, the beneficiary has not responded, then he has lost his right to object to any item in the account. Of course, the beneficiary's failure to respond would not protect a trustee who has acted in a fraudulent manner.

F. *Duty to Make the Trust Property Productive*.

A trustee has a specific duty to make the trust property productive. This means that the trust assets must be invested with the goal that they will produce a reasonable flow of income and a reasonable rate of return for the beneficiary. In general, the appropriate investment strategy will depend on several factors, including the beneficiary's needs, his age and health status, and the size of the trust corpus. A typical investment portfolio for a younger beneficiary in stable health might emphasize long term growth, while a portfolio for an older person whose health is uncertain might emphasize income.

The duty to make the trust productive can pose challenges for the trustee who must consider the special needs of a disabled beneficiary. For example, sometimes when there has been a settlement of an injury case, the beneficiary may desperately need adequate housing and transportation. From the point of view of maximizing returns, however, purchasing housing for the beneficiary does not appear to be a good investment. After all, the beneficiary usually cannot pay market rent and will be not be moving anytime soon, especially if the housing and community services are adequate.

If purchasing housing appears to be a poor investment, then purchasing transportation looks even worse. No trustee is going to make money selling a four-year-old van and replacing it with a new vehicle.

In this situation, the Trustee must look to the overall goal of the Special Needs Trust, which is usually to improve, to the extent possible, the daily life of the disabled beneficiary. In this way, substantial disbursements for a house or specially equipped van can easily be justified. Of course, if the beneficiary's current needs are adequately met, then the trustee should instead invest the trust assets in ways that will provide a reasonable rate of return and reasonable growth for the trust.

What happens if the trustee violates her fiduciary duty?

If trustee violates her fiduciary duty, then she may be liable to the beneficiaries for her breach of trust. A breach of trust may be *intentional* or *negligent*.

A trustee is generally liable for any *intentional* breach of trust, such as stealing money from the trust, or borrowing money from the trust at low or no interest, or failing to pay back money she has borrowed.

A trustee may also be liable for any *negligent* breach of trust, for example, if she hires an unqualified investment advisor, or fails to file tax returns on a timely basis and thereby incurs interest and penalties, or allows insurance to lapse, causing loss to the trust. To remedy the breach of trust, the trustee may have to reimburse the trust's losses from her personal assets.

Some trusts include an *exculpatory clause*. This is a legal term for a provision that limits the trustee's liability. An exculpatory clause is designed to protect the trustee. An exculpatory clause might say that if a trustee acts in good faith, then she will not be liable for any action that she takes or fails to take. However, an exculpatory clause may not protect a trustee who acts in bad faith or with gross negligence.

If a trust does not include an exculpatory clause, then the standard to which a trustee is held depends upon the law of the state that governs the trust. In this situation, the trustee should consult local counsel for advice and direction.

Investments

What standards govern the trustee's investment activities?

Since every trust is different, the trustee must carefully review the investment and management sections of the trust instrument to learn what standards will govern her activities. In Massachusetts, trustees must comply with the Prudent Investor Act (M.G.L. Ch. 203C), unless there is specific language in the trust instrument that exempts the trustee. Trustees outside of Massachusetts should work with an attorney to learn what standards and practices may apply in their own state. The Massachusetts Prudent Investor Act, which is located in the Appendix, covers the following topics:

A. *Specific Management Standards in Trust Instruments*. The Prudent Investor Rule may be "expanded, restricted, eliminated, or otherwise altered by the provisions of a trust." M.G.L. Ch. 203C § 2(b). In other words, if the trust contains specific investment and management standards, then those standards will govern, and a trustee will not be liable to the beneficiaries if she acts in reliance on the specific directions of the trust. For example, some Special Needs Trusts state that the trustee must purchase only low or no risk investments, such as bank CD's,

Treasury bills, money market funds, and so forth. Since the trustee *must* follow these instructions, she will not be liable to the beneficiaries if the trust earnings are below average or because she has failed to diversify the trust portfolio (see section D below).

However, if the trust contains no such specific standards, then the Massachusetts trustee must comply with the Prudent Investor Act. M.G.L. Ch. 203C § 2(a).

B. *Standard of Care.* The trustee must "invest and manage trust assets as a prudent investor would, considering the purpose, terms, and other circumstances of the trust…(using) reasonable care, skill, and caution." In other words, the trustee fulfills her fiduciary duty as long as she acts reasonably under all of the circumstances.

The statute lists eight factors that a trustee must consider in investing and managing trust assets (assuming that those factors are relevant to the particular trust or to its beneficiaries):

1. general economic conditions;
2. the possible effect of inflation or deflation;
3. the expected tax consequences of investment decisions or strategies;
4. the role that each investment or course of actions plays within the overall trust portfolio;
5. the expected total return from income and the appreciation of capital;
6. other resources of the beneficiaries;
7. need for liquidity, regularity of income, and preservation or appreciation of capital; and
8. an asset's special relationship or special value, if any, to the purposes of the trust or to one of the beneficiaries.

M.G.L. Ch. 203C § 3.

C. *The Trust Portfolio as a Whole.* A Trustee's investment and management decisions respecting individual assets "shall be considered in the context of the trust portfolio as a whole, as part of an overall investment strategy reasonably suited to the trust." M.G.L. Ch. 203C § 3(b). In other words, the trustee's decision to purchase, retain, or sell a *particular* asset cannot be challenged by the beneficiaries as long as the *overall* portfolio is reasonable.

D. _Diversification of Assets._ A trustee must "reasonably diversify the investments of the trust _unless, under the circumstances, it is prudent not to do so_" (emphasis added). M.G.L. Ch. 203C § 4. There is a preference that the trust assets be held in a variety of stocks, bonds, cash, and other types of investments. However, the law also recognizes that there may be sound business reasons for the trustee to hold assets in only one or two types of investments. Here, the trustee who "invests" the trust funds in housing or transportation for the disabled beneficiary will find support for her decision. These types of "investments" may do little to augment the trust fund or enhance its productivity in the traditional sense, but may nevertheless enrich the daily life of the beneficiary, which, after all, is the purpose of the Special Needs Trust.

E. _Initial Duty to Review Trust Assets._ The trustee must "within a reasonable time after accepting a trusteeship or receiving trust assets…review the trust assets and make and implement decisions concerning the retention and disposition of assets." M.G.L.203C § 5. In order to comply with this obligation, we suggest that a financial advisor be retained to evaluate the initial asset allocation and review the portfolio at least annually thereafter to assure the appropriateness of investments.

F. _The Duty of Loyalty._ The trustee must "invest and manage the trust assets solely in the interest of the beneficiaries." M.G.L. 203C § 6. The duty of loyalty (or the fiduciary duty) is discussed earlier in this chapter. Essentially, the duty of loyalty prohibits the trustee from becoming personally involved in any financial transactions with the trust, such as borrowing money, making loans to her family or friends, or lending money to the trust. These transactions (called self-dealing), in addition to being a breach of the trustee's fiduciary duty, are a violation of law, and must be avoided.

G. _The Duty of Impartiality._ A trustee must "act impartially in investing and managing the trust assets, taking into account any different interests of the beneficiaries." M.G.L. 203C § 7. This is not usually an issue with most Special Needs Trusts because there is only one lifetime beneficiary, and thus the trustee does not have to deal with the competing interests of other lifetime beneficiaries.

H. _Costs._ The costs incurred in investing and managing the trust assets must be "appropriate and reasonable in relation to the assets, purpose of the trust, and the skills of the trustee." M.G.L. 203 § 8. While relatively high costs may be justified for a large trust, a trustee administering a modest trust for a person with disabilities must be mindful that the total costs related to her fees, her financial advisor's fees, broker's commissions, etc., are not unreasonable.

I. *Delegation of Duties*. A trustee may delegate investment and management activities to advisors so long as she uses reasonable care, skill, and caution in: (a) selecting the agent; (b) establishing the scope and terms of the delegation, consistent with the terms and purposes of the trust; and (c) periodically reviewing the agent's actions. M.G.L. Ch. 203C § 10. In most cases, a trustee who complies with this delegation rule will not be liable to the beneficiaries for the poor judgment or misconduct of her agents.

CHAPTER 11

GLOSSARY OF TERMS

Account/Accounting: A summary of financial activity for a trust for a specific period of time, usually one year.

Administrative Expenses: The costs associated with operating a trust, typically including professional fees, trustee's fees, etc.

Assets: Also referred to as "resources" in the SSI program. Items of value owned by an SSI recipient including money, stocks, bonds, real estate, personal property, etc. SSI classifies assets as either countable or non-countable. One can have only limited countable assets to qualify for SSI or other means-tested programs.

Beneficiary: The person or persons whom a trust is intended to benefit.

Code of Federal Regulations (C.F.R.): A compilation of the regulations promulgated by the relevant federal agency having jurisdiction over a program. For instance, the Department of Housing and Urban Development (HUD) promulgates regulations about rental assistance programs and publishes them in the Code of Federal Regulations.

Code of Massachusetts Regulations (C.M.R.): A compilation of regulations promulgated by the relevant Massachusetts agency having jurisdiction over a program. For instance, the Massachusetts Division of Medical Assistance promulgates regulations about the MassHealth program and publishes them in the Code of Massachusetts Regulations.

Co-Trustee: A person named by the Grantor, Settlor, or Donor of a trust to administer the trust with another trustee for the beneficiary of the trust.

Countable Asset: A resource (item of value) that is considered when determining if one is eligible for a means-tested program such as SSI.

Corpus: Assets held in a trust.

Disability: As defined by the Social Security Administration in the SSI and SSDI Programs, "the inability to engage in substantial gainful activity due to a medical impairment or combination of impairments that can be expected to last for a continuous period of twelve months or result in death."

Distribution: A payment by a trustee of a trust to or for the benefit of the beneficiary.

Donor: The creator of a trust. Donor, Grantor, and Settlor are synonymous. The Donor is usually, but not always, the person who funds the trust. See definition of Grantor.

Earned Income: Income that is earned by an individual through work or labor, as opposed to unearned or passive income, which comes from investments or rents.

Federal Benefit Rate (F.B.R.): The amount the federal government contributes to an individual's SSI grant. In 2005, the amount is $579 per month. Most states supplement the federal benefit rate, resulting in larger payments for the SSI recipient.

Fiduciary: A person who has a duty to act primarily for another person's benefit. A trustee is a fiduciary.

Grantor: The creator of a trust. Grantor, Donor, and Settlor are synonymous. The Grantor is usually, but not always, the person who funds the trust.

HUD: The Department of Housing and Urban Development. HUD administers rental assistance programs like Section 8.

Impairment Related Work Expenses (IRWE's): Certain expenses incurred by a person with disabilities that allow him to work, e.g., specialized transportation, job supervision.

Independent Trustee: A trustee who is not subject to the control of a beneficiary of a trust and who has no beneficial interest in the trust property.

In-kind Income: Food, shelter, or something a recipient of public benefits can use to obtain any of these items.

Irrevocable Trust: A trust whose terms cannot be changed.

MassHealth: The Medicaid Program in Massachusetts.

Medicaid: A federal- and state-funded health insurance program for low- and middle-income individuals (and their families) and for persons with disabilities. In Massachusetts, Medicaid is called MassHealth.

Medicare: The health insurance program associated with Social Security. Medicare is not means-tested. People receiving SSDI are eligible to receive Medicare after they have received benefits for two years, with the exception of people having amyotrophic lateral sclerosis (ALS), who are eligible for Medicare contemporaneously with their SSDI eligibility.

Needs-based Program: A program that has financial criteria for eligibility, such as the SSI or Medicaid programs, for which one must have limited assets and income to qualify. See Means-tested program.

Plan for Achieving Self-Support (PASS): A program, which must be pre-approved by the Social Security Administration, that will allow an SSI recipient to earn more income or own more assets than normally allowed by SSI, as a means to achieve self-support.

Program Operations Manual System (POMS): It contains the Social Security Administration's internal guidelines and rules for administering the SSI program. It is now available on line at www.ssa.gov.

Principal: The capital (or corpus) of a trust, in contrast to the "income" or "interest" the principal earns when invested.

Revocable Trust: A trust that can be amended, revoked, or terminated.

Resources: Items of value owned by an SSI recipient including money, stocks, bonds, real estate, personal property, etc. SSI classifies resources as either countable or non-countable. One can have only limited countable resources to qualify for SSI or other means-tested programs.

Section 8: A rental assistance program sponsored by HUD and administered by local housing authorities. Typically, a person eligible for SSI pays rent based on his income, and the housing authority pays the balance of the rent to the landlord.

Settlor: The creator of a trust. Settlor, Donor, and Settlor are synonymous. The Settlor is usually, but not always, the person who funds the trust.

Social Security Administration (SSA): The federal agency that administers the SSI and SSDI programs.

Self-settled Trust: A trust created by a person with disabilities for his own benefit, into which he places his own assets. Compare to a third party trust.

Special Needs Trust (SNT): A trust which holds funds for the benefit of a disabled beneficiary that is designed to protect, maintain or achieve eligibility for means-tested public benefits programs like SSI or Medicaid, while at the same time providing a source of funds to meet the beneficiary's ongoing needs.

SSDI (Social Security Disability Income): A federal program that pays monthly cash benefits to workers with disabilities (and their dependents) who have paid Social Security taxes on their earnings. SSDI is not a means-tested program.

SSI (Supplemental Security Income): A means-tested federal benefit program that pays monthly cash benefits to aged, blind, or disabled individuals who have limited income and financial resources.

Substantial Gainful Activity (SGA): A component of the Social Security's definition of disability for the SSDI and SSI programs. Disability for adults in the SSI and SSDI programs is defined as being unable to engage in SGA due to a medical or physical impairment or combination of impairments. In 2005, the SSA has determined that, absent mitigating circumstances, anyone earning over $830 per month ($1,380 if blind) is engaged in substantial gainful activity.

Successor Trustee: A trustee who succeeds the initial trustee or trustees named in a trust.

Supplemental Needs Trust: See Special Needs Trust.

TAFDC (Transitional Aid to Families with Dependent Children): A means-tested benefit program to assist dependent children. In Massachusetts, TAFDC is administered by the Division of Transitional Assistance.

Third Party Trust: A trust created for a beneficiary by someone other than the beneficiary, and funded with that person's (or another person's assets). Compare to a self-settled trust.

Trust: An agreement between a Settlor, Grantor, or Donor and a Trustee to administer funds for the benefit of one or more beneficiaries pursuant to the terms of the agreement.

Trustee: The person or entity appointed or required by law to execute or administer a trust.

Unearned Income: Income that is not derived from one's personal labor, i.e., investment income, interest on a bank account, etc.

CHAPTER 12

WHERE TO GO FOR HELP

The websites and publications listed below may assist the reader who wants to know more.

WEBSITES:

www.nichcy.org A national website listing services, programs, and providers that assist people with disabilities.

www.fedstats.gov Contains federal statistics, including current federal poverty levels.

www.huduser.org/datasets/pdrdatas.html Website of the U.S. Department of Housing and Urban Development (HUD); contains the section 8 payment standards for public housing authorities in all fifty states.

www.hudclips.org HUD website that contains useful information on subsidized housing programs.

www.huduser.org/datasets/il.html HUD website that contains the section 8 income limits.

www.lawlib.state.ma.us Contains current Massachusetts laws and regulations.

www.ssa.gov.org Official website of the Social Security Administration. Contains most federal disability laws and regulations, including the POMS.

www.state.ma.us/mod/msdislaw.html Compendium of all disability laws in Massachusetts.

www.mass.gov/dma The Massachusetts Division of Medical Assistance website. Contains information on MassHealth programs.

www.tacinc.org Website of the Technical Assistance Collaborative, Inc. Contains helpful information on subsidized housing, including several publications.

www.800ageinfo.com The Massachusetts Prescription Advantage Program website.

PUBLICATIONS:

An Advocate's Guide to Surviving the SSI System. By Linda L. Landry, et al. Disability Law Center, Massachusetts Law Reform Institute, and Massachusetts Continuing Legal Institute, Inc. (2000). Also known as "the Yellow Book." An invaluable resource guide to SSI financial and disability rules. Highly recommended, reasonably priced.

Benefits Management for Working People with Disabilities. By Neighborhood Legal Services. Can be ordered on NLS website, www.nls.org.

Estate Planning for the Aging or Incapacitated Client in Massachusetts: Protecting Legal Rights, Preserving Resources and Providing Health Care Options. By Massachusetts Continuing Legal Education, Inc. Edited by Donald N. Freedman and Emily S. Starr. (Rev. ed. 1998, supplemented 2002) Highly recommended.

The Law of Trusts. By Scott and Fratcher (Little, Brown, 4th ed., 1987) Eleven-volume set. Available at most law libraries.

Loring: A Trustee's Handbook. By Loring and Rounds (Aspen Publishers, Inc., 2001). Useful, one-volume handbook on trust administration.

The Red Book on Employment. Publication 64-030 of the Social Security Administration: Guide to Social Security work-related rules and regulations. Can be found on the SSA website (www.ssa.gov.org) or ordered by mail.

Section 8 Made Simple. By Technical Assistance Collaborative, Inc. (2002). Excellent reader-friendly guide to the Section 8 program. Can be obtained from TAC's website (www.tacinc.org).

APPENDIX

1. Acceptance of Trustee

2. Declination of Trustee

3. Resignation of Trustee

4. Account (Three Schedules)

5. Account (Six Schedules)

6. First and Final Account

7. Assent to Account

8. Prudent Investor Act

9. SSI Payment Standards (2005)

Form 1
Acceptance of Trustee

THE JOHN DOE SPECIAL NEEDS TRUST

ACCEPTANCE

I, _____(name), of _____(address), being the designated successor trustee of the above captioned trust, a trust instrument dated _____, do hereby accept the appointment as trustee of that trust.

Witness my hand and seal this _____ day of _____ 200_.

_____

Commonwealth of Massachusetts

County: _____   Date: _____

Then appeared before me the above named _____ and acknowledged that s/he signed the foregoing as his/her free act and deed.

_____
Notary Public
My commission expires:

Form 2
Resignation of Trustee

THE JOHN DOE SPECIAL NEEDS TRUST

RESIGNATION

I, _____ (name), of _____(address), being the trustee of the above captioned trust, do hereby resign my office as trustee.

Witness my hand and seal this _____ day of _____, 200_.

_____

Commonwealth of Massachusetts

County: _____   Date: _____

Then appeared before me the above named _____and acknowledged that s/he signed the foregoing as his/her free act and deed.

_____
Notary Public
My commission expires:

Form 3
Declination of Trustee

THE JOHN DOE SPECIAL NEEDS TRUST

DECLINATION

I, _____(name), of _____ (address) being
the designated successor of the above captioned trust, a trust instrument dated
_____ do hereby decline to serve in that capacity.

Witness my hand and seal this _____ day of _____200_.

_____

Commonwealth of Massachusetts

County: _____   Date: _____

Then appeared before me the above named _____ and acknowledged
that s/he signed the foregoing as his/her free act and deed.

_____
Notary Public
My commission expires:

Form 4
Account—Three Schedules

ACCOUNT

FIRST ACCOUNT OF JANE DOE AS TRUSTEE OF THE JOHN DOE SPECIAL NEEDS TRUST

January 1, 2001, to December 31, 2001

Schedule A

Income

Number	Date	Payee/Purpose	Amount
1.	Beginning balance		$20,014.20
2.	Various interest on Medford Bank Account #12345		$117.18
3.	02/07/00	Payment on Promissory Note	$575.88
4.	05/25/00	Payment on Promissory Note	$575.88
5.	06/01/00	Payment on Promissory Note	$575.88
6.	07/06/00	Payment on Promissory Note	$575.88
7.	08/21/00	Payment on Promissory Note	$575.88
8.	09/01/00	Payment on Promissory Note	$575.88
9.	10/30/00	Payment on Promissory Note	$575.88

10.	11/07/00	Payment on Promissory Note	$575.88
11.	12/15/00	Payment on Promissory Note	$575.88
		TOTAL	**$25,314.30**

Schedule B

Payments

Number	Date	Description	Amount
1.		Bank charges (3)	$10.04
2.	02/10/00	John Doe (distribution)	$1,789.96
3.	04/06/00	IRS (1999 Income Tax)	$126.00
4.	04/05/00	Commonwealth of Mass. (1998 Tax)	$12.00
5.	05/25/00	Cynthia Trustee (trustee fee)	$500.00
6.	05/25/00	H&R Block (tax preparation)	$250.00
7.	07/27/00	Alternative Leisure (summer vacation for John Doe)	$1,250.00
8.	12/10/00	John Doe (holiday gifts)	$250.00
		TOTAL	**$4,188.00**

Schedule C

Balance

1. Schedule A	$25,314.30
2. Schedule B	$4,188.00
3. Schedule C	$21,126.30

Reconciliation

Medford Bank Money Market Acct. on 12/13/00 $21,126.30

Form 5
Account—Six Schedules

SECOND ACCOUNT OF JANE DOE AS TRUSTEE OF THE JOHN DOE SPECIAL NEEDS TRUST
January 1, 2002–December 31, 2002

SCHEDULE A

Principal balance per next prior account	$110,000

1. Loss on sale of 100 shares of AT&T stock
    on May 1, 2003

    Book value: $23.00
    Sale price: $17.87 $513

TOTAL SCHEDULE A	**$109,487**

SCHEDULE B

1. Trustee compensation	$1,200
2. Camp Horizons (summer vacation for John Doe)	$2,300
3. Jane Doe (Guardianship fees)	$1,800
TOTAL SCHEDULE B	**$5,300**

SCHEDULE C

	Book Value	Market Value
1. U.S. Treasury Bill Account	$47,500	$48,100
2. Middlesex Bank Money Mkt Acct	$11,000	$11,000
3. Vanguard Sh Term Corp Bond Fund	$40,500	$40,750
4. Fleet CD Account	$10,000	$10,300
5. Cash on hand	$1,200	$1,200
TOTAL SCHEDULE C	**$110,200**	**$111,350**

SCHEDULE D

Income Balance per next prior Account	$1,100
1. Interest on U.S. Treasury Account	$1,100
2. Interest on Middlesex Bank Account	$63
3. Dividends on Vanguard Sh Term Corp. Bond Fund	$1,620
4. Interest on Fleet CD Account	$250
TOTAL SCHEDULE D	**$4,133**

SCHEDULE E

1. John Doe (cash disbursements)	$250
2. Trustee compensation	$1,200
3. Miscellaneous distributions on behalf of John Doe (holiday gifts, program fees, recreation costs, Cape Cod beach trip, Red Sox tickets)	$1,500
TOTAL SCHEDULE E	**$2,950**

SCHEDULE F

1. Income balance on hand	$1,183

Form 6
Account—Final

SIXTH AND FINAL ACCOUNT OF JANE DOE, TRUSTEE OF THE JOHN DOE SPECIAL NEEDS TRUST

January 1, 2001 through September 30, 2001

Schedule A

1.	Balance from next prior account	$81,941.59
2.	Interest on Eastern Bank Acct #1234	$47.11
3.	Proceeds from sale of personal property	$720.00
	TOTAL	$82,708.70

Schedule B

Number	Date	Payee/Purpose	Amount
1.	06/01/01	McDonalds Funeral Home	$595.00
2.	06/01/01	Mt. Auburn Cemetery	$450.00
3.	06/05/01	St. Paul's Church (donation)	$75.00
4.	07/01/01	Mass. General Hospital (medical bill)	$61.40
5.	09/01/01	Jane Doe (trustee's fee)	$750.00
6.	09/02/01	Best Drug (prescription meds)	$81.00
7.	09/15/01	Richard Doe (distribution)	$25,113.76

8.	09/15/01	Margaret Doe (distribution)	$25,113.77
9.	09/15/01	Samuel Doe (distribution)	$25,113.77
TOTAL			**$82,708.70**

Schedule C

1. Schedule A	$82,708.70
2. Schedule B	$82,708.70
3. Schedule C	none

Form 7
Assent

THE JOHN DOE SPECIAL NEEDS TRUST

ASSENT TO THE FIRST AND FINAL ACCOUNT OF THE TRUSTEE

In the matter of the JOHN DOE SPECIAL NEEDS TRUST, I, _____ (name), of _____ (address) being a party interested in the above matter, acknowledge receipt of the sum of $_____ as a final distribution to me, in full satisfaction of all claims under that trust. I further assent to the First and Final account of the Trustee.

Date: _____

_____   _____

Witness

MASSACHUSETTS GENERAL LAWS
CHAPTER 203C. PRUDENT INVESTMENT.

Section 1. This chapter shall be known as and may be cited as the Massachusetts Prudent Investor Act.

Section 2. (a) Except as provided in subsection (b), a trustee who invests and manages trust assets shall owe a duty to the beneficiaries of a trust to comply with the prudent investor rule set forth in this chapter.

(b) The prudent investor rule may be expanded, restricted, eliminated or otherwise altered by the provisions of a trust. A trustee shall not be liable to a beneficiary to the extent that the trustee acted in reasonable reliance on the provisions of the trust.

Section 3. (a) A trustee shall invest and manage trust assets as a prudent investor would, considering the purposes, terms, and other circumstances of the trust, including those set forth in subsection (c). In satisfying this standard, the trustee shall exercise reasonable care, skill, and caution.

(b) A trustee's investment and management decisions respecting individual assets shall be considered in the context of the trust portfolio as a part of an overall investment strategy reasonably suited to the trust.

(c) Among circumstances that the trustee shall consider in investing and managing trust asset are such of the following as are relevant to the trust or its beneficiaries:

(1) general economic conditions;

(2) the possible effect of inflation or deflation;

(3) The expected tax consequences of investment decisions or strategies;

(4) the role that each investment or course of action plays within the overall trust portfolio;

(5) the expected total return from income and the appreciation of capital;

(6) other resources of the beneficiaries;

(7) needs for liquidity, regularity of income, and preservation or appreciation of capital; and

(8) an asset's special relationship or special value, if any, to the purposes of the trust or to one of the beneficiaries.

(d) A trustee shall make a reasonable effort to verify facts relevant to the investment and management of trust assets.

(e) A trustee may invest in any kind of property or type of investment consistent with the standards of this chapter.

(f) A trustee who has special skills or expertise, or is named trustee in reliance upon the trustee's representation that the trustee has such special skills or expertise, shall have a duty to use such special skills or expertise.

Section 4. A trustee shall reasonably diversify the investments of the trust unless, under the circumstances, it is prudent not to do so.

Section 5. Within a reasonable time after accepting a trusteeship or receiving trust assets, a trustee shall review the trust assets and make and implement decisions concerning the retention and disposition of assets, in order to bring the trust portfolio into compliance with the purposes, terms, and the other circumstances of the trust, and with the requirements of this chapter.

Section 6. A trustee shall invest and manage the trust assets solely in the interest of the beneficiaries.

Section 7. If a trust has two or more beneficiaries, the trustee shall act impartially in investing and managing the trust assets, taking into account any differing interests of the beneficiaries.

Section 8. In investing and managing trust assets, a trustee shall incur only costs that are appropriate and reasonable in relation to the assets, the purpose of the trust, and the skills of the trustee.

Section 9. Compliance with the prudent investor rule shall be determined in light of the facts and circumstances existing at the time of a trustee's decision or action.

Section 10. (a) A trustee may delegate investment and management functions if it is prudent to do so. A trustee shall exercise reasonable care, skill and caution in:

(1) selecting an agent;

(2) establishing the scope and terms of the delegation, consistent with the purposes and terms of the trust; and

(3) periodically reviewing the agent's actions in order to monitor the agent's performance and compliance with the terms of the delegation.

(b) In performing a delegated function, an agent shall owe a duty to the trust to exercise reasonable care to comply with the terms of the delegation.

(c) A trustee who complies with the requirements of subsection (a) shall not be liable to the beneficiaries or to the trust for the decisions or actions of the agent to whom the function was delegated.

(d) By accepting the delegation of trust functions from the trustee of a trust that is subject to the laws of the commonwealth, an agent submits to the jurisdiction of the courts of the commonwealth.

Section 11. The following terms or comparable language in the provisions of a trust, unless otherwise limited or modified, authorize any investment or strategy permitted under this chapter and shall not be interpreted to be a restriction, elimination, or other alteration or the prudent investor rule for purposes of subsection (b) of section 2: "investments permissible by law for investment of trust funds," "legal investments", "authorized investments", "using the judgment and care under the circumstances then prevailing that persons of prudence, discretion, and intelligence exercise in the management of their own affairs, not in regard to speculation but in regard to the permanent disposition of their funds, considering the probable income as well as the probable safety of their capital", "prudent man rule", "prudent trustee rule", "prudent person rule", and "prudent investor rule".

2005 SSI PAYMENT LEVELS (MASSACHUSETTS)

LIVING ARRANGEMENT: FULL COST OF LIVING

	Benefit Type	Federal Benefit	State Supplement	TOTAL
INDIVIDUAL	Aged	$579.00	$128.82	$707.82
	Disabled	$579.00	$114.39	$693.39
	Blind	$579.00	$149.74	$728.74
MEMBER OF A COUPLE	Aged	$434.00	$100.86	$523.86
	Disabled	$423.00	$90.03	$535.03
	Blind	$434.00	$294.74	$728.74

LIVING ARRANGEMENT: SHARED LIVING

	Benefit Type	Federal Benefit	State Supplement	TOTAL
INDIVIDUAL	Aged	$579.00	$39.26	$618.26
	Disabled	$579.00	$30.40	$604.40
	Blind	$579.00	$149.74	$728.74
MEMBER OF A COUPLE	Aged	$434.50	$100.86	$535.86
	Disabled	$434.00	$90.03	$524.03
	Blind	$434.00	$294.74	$728.74

LIVING ARRANGEMENT: HOUSEHOLD OF ANOTHER

	Benefit Type	Federal Benefit	State Supplement	TOTAL
INDIVIDUAL	Aged	$386.00	$104.36	**$490.36**
	Disabled	$386.00	$87.58	**$473.58**
	Blind	$386.00	$342.74	**$728.74**
MEMBER OF A COUPLE	Aged	$289.67	$107.90	**$397.57**
	Disabled	$289.67	$97.09	**$386.76**
	Blind	$289.67	$439.07	**$728.74**

LIVING ARRANGEMENT: LICENSED REST HOME

	Benefit Type	Federal Benefit	State Supplement	TOTAL
INDIVIDUAL	Aged	$579.00	$293.00	**$872.00**
	Disabled	$579.00	$293.00	**$872.00**
	Blind	$579.00	$149.74	**$728.74**
MEMBER OF A COUPLE	Aged	$434.50	$437.50	**$872.00**
	Disabled	$434.50	$437.50	**$872.00**
	Blind	$434.50	$294.24	**$728.74**

LIVING ARRANGEMENT: ASSISTED LIVING

	Benefit Type	Federal Benefit	State Supplement	TOTAL
INDIVIDUAL	Aged	$579.00	$454.00	$1033.00
	Disabled	$579.00	$454.00	$1033.00
	Blind	$579.00	$454.00	$1033.00
MEMBER OF A COUPLE	Aged	$434.50	$340.50	$775.00
	Disabled	$434.50	$340.50	$775.00
	Blind	$434.50	$340.50	$775.00

INDEX

978-0-595-33106-2
0-595-33106-8

Printed in the United States
215620BV00005B/54/A